THE

ELEGANT PROCESS

The Elegant Process

The Guide to

Enhanced Quality and Reduced Costs

JASON KILGORE

Copyright© 2010 by ProSpeed Results LLC

All rights reserved. No part of this book may be used or reproduced in any manner without prior written consent of the publisher, except as provided by the United States of America copyright law.

Published by ProSpeed Results LLC, Newport News, Virginia
Cover design by GLP Designs
Photo by Art Louis Photography

Printed in the United States of America

ISBN: 978-0-615-35718-8

Bulk purchases of this book may be made by contacting the publisher at www.prospeedresults.com or through Executive Business Approach at www.ebapproach.com.

Author contact information:
www.jasonkilgore.com
jasonkilgore@aol.com

Library of Congress Control Number: 2010903120

Kilgore, Jason T., 1973-
The Elegant Process: The Guide to Enhanced Quality and Reduced Costs / by Jason Kilgore

Robin & Madison

Mom, Dad, Jeremy, Sara

The Elegant Process

The Guide to

Enhanced Quality and Reduced Costs

Contents

INTRODUCTION 1

PROCESS THINKING

Chapter 1: The Elegant Process 7

Chapter 2: A Different View.. 15

Chapter 3: The Intersection of Value, Cost, and Quality....... 25

Chapter 4: Adding Value 35

Chapter 5: The Seven Wastes 45

PROCESS DESIGN

Chapter 6: Build the Process.. 55

Chapter 7: Shrink the Process 65

Chapter 8: Get Rhythm, Part 1 – Tempo 75

Chapter 9: Get Rhythm, Part 2 – Synchronicity 81

Chapter 10: Go with Flow... 91

SUSTAINING THE PROCESS

Chapter 11: Error-proof the Process.............................103

Chapter 12: Technology and the Visual Workplace.............115

Chapter 13: The Ideal Process.............................125

Chapter 14: The Way Forward.............................137

Introduction

The field of process design and improvement captivated my attention many years ago. Though my first forays were in manufacturing and product development, I kept thinking to myself that these principles could do so much more than just squeeze a couple of cents out of the cost of each widget. I became increasingly intrigued by the coordinated movement and exchange of resources. This process, if done optimally, produces a benefit among the entities involved in the exchange. The more my experience broadens, the more I am convinced that process improvement principles work across industries, business models, and cultures.

What makes a business worthwhile and profitable is its ability to resolve the conflict between meeting the needs of the producer (cost control) and the needs of the consumer (quality of product or service). This conflict exists primarily due to the highly dynamic customer attitudes toward and expectations for the products and services they consume. On one hand, consumers want the most cutting-edge convenience available; on the other hand, there is a limit on what they are willing to pay for such an item. On yet a third hand, consumers want to be completely satisfied with the quality of the goods and services they receive. This dilemma gives rise to the axiom, "You can have the best price, highest quality, or fastest delivery — pick two."

Many process improvement methodologies are packaged and sold with the promise of solving this dilemma. Most are useful if you have the time and patience to navigate the intricacies of these largely academic frameworks.

Rule #1: Think process, not problems. What I have found, and thus one motivation for writing this book, is that many improvements can be made simply by defining and analyzing problems in terms of process flow. The approach laid forth in this book takes many of the principles from the most highly noted process improvement strategies and merges them into a straightforward guide on how to resolve most nagging business issues. I have personally used this strategy to deliver millions of dollars in cost savings over the last fifteen years.

Rule #2: Simple is better. The second motivation for writing this book is my realization that many problem solving and process improvement methodologies are intimidating to even the most astute business and operations professionals. Though useful and meaningful, jargon such as *jidoka* or *standard deviation* immediately raise the anxiety level of many savvy leaders. Demonstrating these proven principles in our everyday experiences can easily be accomplished without assigning lofty terminology to every concept.

Rule #3: Start at the beginning. The third motivation came to me at the conclusion of a recent training session. As a colleague and I completed several days' worth of training, she looked at me and said, "This was all great information, but now what?" In other words, we learned many terms and concepts, but she was still unsure how to kick start process improvement efforts within her own organization. I recognized at that point that an effective problem-solving strategy must detail techniques on exactly how to begin the process improvement effort.

My purpose is to deliver a concise and understandable process improvement and problem solving approach that is accessible, free from excessive jargon, and easy to follow and execute. This approach is not intended to resurrect businesses from the brink of disaster. Such action would require many more tools and is well outside the scope of this book. However, the framework set forth in this book can help good organizations become better, make marginal businesses profitable, and enhance the quality of products and services, regardless of industry or sector.

Many highly technical and complex process-related issues can be resolved without formal education and training. They merely require a simple, yet thorough analysis of what the current process is, what is most needed, and what compromises can be made. These three elements, when considered separately and as a part of the larger system, often lead to a cost-effective and high-quality solution. The solution which completely resolves the cost-quality dilemma is *the elegant process.*

Effective improvement efforts require the problem to be viewed in two lights. First, we must consider the value our business brings to the marketplace. As we will learn, every step in our business processes either adds to or detracts from the value we are trying to deliver to the consumer. A conscious evaluation of this value stream and how it flows from the producer to the consumer will determine the success of our improvement endeavor.

It follows that problems must be viewed as process failures caused by the improper execution of predefined tasks. This perspective allows us to focus on the cause-and-effect relationship between what we want and what we get, which are not always the same. Solving process-related issues requires the examination of the gap between the actual performance and the expected performance. Addressing the

INTRODUCTION

causes of this gap directly will produce a more effective and efficient future process.

Before jumping right into the book, consider the following process for solving problems:

1. Draw the current process as it is.
2. Consider the value of the process.
3. Identify wasted time and effort.
4. Develop the ideal process.
5. Compare the actual and ideal processes.
6. Formulate the elegant process.
7. Make the necessary changes.

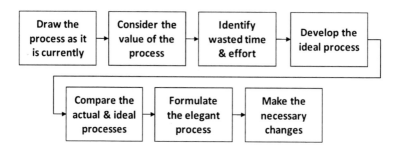

As you read this book, take time to evaluate the processes and systems in your own surroundings. What are those issues that erode profits or tarnish quality? Successful businesses are able to identify and correct those errors before they cause catastrophic failures. Use the principles in this book to tweak or redesign current systems. Challenge conventional thinking and organizational inertia. Decide that good enough is no longer good enough. Use the elegant process to enhance quality and reduce cost in your organization!

Chapter 1: The Elegant Process

"Simplicity, carried to an extreme,
becomes elegance."

– Jon Franklin

I followed conventional wisdom. I watered daily. I seeded in the fall. Yet, summer after summer, my lawn turned brown and was overtaken by weeds. In the fall, I killed the weeds, prepared the soil, sowed the most expensive grass seed I could find, fertilized, and watered religiously. The results were always the same — beautiful green grass in the winter and spring. But by June, my lawn was a complete wasteland. To add insult to injury, my good-natured neighbor across the street had the greenest grass I had ever seen. Indeed, the grass was greener on the other side.

I'm a smart guy, I thought to myself. *I'm an engineer, inventor, and problem-solver. Why can't I have green grass in August?* I wrestled with this question for years. Then, one day, it hit me. There must be a significant gap between *my* way and *the right* way to grow a lush green lawn. ***The result was wrong because my process was wrong!*** And, if I wanted to have green grass, my grass-growing process was going to have to change.

One day, the small voice in the back of my mind reminded me of what I have always known: *quality outcomes are the result of a well-designed process.* I set out on a winter-long quest to identify the right type of grass for my yard, the proper sowing technique, the appropriate soil preparation, and optimal watering method. When spring came, my project began. I implemented my well-designed and carefully thought-out plan: testing the soil, installing a sprinkler system, spreading compost, and sowing the seed. My grass emerged and held on through July and August. By summer's end, I still had green grass. I had finally put all the right pieces together at the right time and in the right place. I had a process. I had confirmed that success was the result of the correct process and not of hard work alone.

Successful businesses are built on their ability to implement and sustain reliable and efficient processes. Orchestrating the efforts of employees, whether ten or ten thousand, requires a deliberate blueprint at the most basic level of the organization. These blueprints, or processes, describe the core functions of the workforce, communicating to each person what to do, how to do it, and when to do it. More than just a business plan, these working-level details are needed to coordinate and regulate the performance of the human efforts within the business environment. *Process* is the mechanism for achieving this complex coordination of the many endeavors within a business.

Processes enable the repeatability of desired outcomes, ensuring quality, in the form of customer satisfaction, and containing cost by preventing mistakes detrimental to bottom line profits. Formally, a process is a series of actions leading to the accomplishment of a goal. A process can have any number of steps, sub-processes, or tasks, each of which contains a number of significant inputs. Each step within a process is preceded and followed by another, building a chain of events moving toward the anticipated conclusion.

A process can be found in any business environment: how employees get paid, how the marketing department buys advertising, or how the fleet of company vehicles is maintained. Stocking, tracking, and selling inventory involve actions taking on the form of a process. All systematic movement within a business relies on process to transfer a product or service from concept to revenue.

When a process flows flawlessly and effortlessly, it is *elegant*. The elegant process delivers a product or service to the consumer without drama, as planned, with complete satisfaction, and at a profit. Non-elegant processes lead to customer complaints, extraneous costs, and employee dissatisfaction. Failed and unreliable processes give rise to the seemingly unending string of firefighting, service recovery, and warranty claims. What breaks this cycle of missed opportunities for success? The answer lies in designing, implementing, and sustaining elegant processes.

Recently, our family decided to take a vacation to Florida. I opted to plan my own vacation using online resources as much as possible. I couldn't help but notice the well-defined and almost musical process involved in purchasing plane tickets. The experience flowed intuitively with a certain rhythm from step to step to step from the first click until the final confirmation. This process was so simple and easy it has become my illustration of choice when describing an elegant process (see Figure 1.1).

Figure 1.1 Purchasing Airline Tickets Online

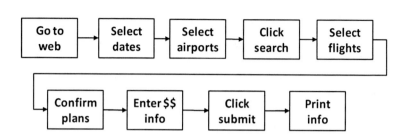

Having confirmed our transportation, I just as efficiently arranged for a rental car and park admissions. Meanwhile, my wife made reservations for breakfast, lunch, and dinner for each day. In the span of minutes, seven days of family bliss were reserved, paid for, and confirmed. Planning our entire vacation was straightforward and process-centric.

What defines an elegant process? An elegant process...

- Targets a clearly delineated outcome or desired result. It is unambiguous in purpose, goal, or objective.

- Delivers a benefit or value to the consumer in a time-efficient manner.

- Is simple and easy to follow, not burdened with unnecessary complication, explanations, or pre-conditions.

- Moves steadily from beginning to end, without unexpected delays or hang-ups.

THE ELEGANT PROCESS

- Consumes only the necessary resources, such as time, labor, transportation, or processing.
- Is free of mistakes, such as poor quality products or services.
- Utilizes technology effectively without inconvenience to the consumer.

When all the actions contained within a process work seamlessly together to bring about a desired and valuable result, the process is deemed elegant. Some elegant processes we now take for granted are a sixty-second drive-through experience, automatic car washes, movies on demand, and e-Bay auctions. These processes have become second nature to most of us. Yet, these seamless exchanges of money and products do not happen by accident. The seamlessness of the interaction is the result of countless hours of process design, time studies, technology application, and marketing research. Would it not be grand if all of our business processes were so elegant?

Take, for example, the nagging invoice your customer neglects to pay despite repeated requests or the seemingly endless delays on information technology integration projects. My personal favorite is the purchase order approval process. Despite our best efforts, the request always seems to get lost or ignored, requiring re-submission. Needless

THE ELEGANT PROCESS

repetition of this procedure serves to delay nearly every purchase. How many millions of dollars are spent due to poorly designed, labor-intensive processes serving only to drain productivity, satisfaction, and profit? Many successful businesses have eliminated both the inconvenience and cost of onerous and erratic tasks by converting haphazard actions into well-designed and elegant processes.

Chapter 2: A Different View

"It's easier to go down a hill than up it,
but the view is much better at the top."

-Henry Ward Beecher

I view the business world differently than most people. My perspective is one viewed through lenses focused on the effective use of process. This view of the business world leads me to certain beneficial conclusions derived from my own research and experience. The following statements about process are essential to enhancing quality and reducing costs within the business environment at large, but more importantly, within your business.

> ## A Different View of Process
>
> **1. Stable, predictable processes are fundamental to value-creating enterprises.**
>
> **2. Well-designed processes return higher quality and lower costs.**
>
> **3. Poor results are a consequence of poor processes, not of a poor workforce.**

**Stable, predictable processes are fundamental to value-creating enterprises**. In the following chapters, we will learn to develop elegant processes by creating stable and predictable processes. At the heart of every process is the predictability of its outcome. Imagine how devastated your business would become if FedEx were not stable and predictable. Stable and reliable — the right package going to the right place. Much of our business depends on the stability of FedEx's processes. We also depend on FedEx being predictable. What would happen if the 10AM delivery arrived randomly throughout the day's twenty-four hours? While FedEx is not perfect, it is adequately predictable insofar as the promise of 10AM delivery means 10AM and we can make reasonable plans based on a package arriving by 10AM. The value to us as the consumer is in FedEx's ability to control its delivery process. In so doing, they provide a meaningful and practical service. Ultimately, only stable and predictable processes are of any value.

Well-designed processes return higher quality and lower costs. Chapter 3 will explore more deeply the interaction between cost and quality. Well-designed processes benefit the consumer by providing a high-quality product delivered with a meaningful and positive experience. But the benefit to the consumer is only half the equation. It also means the producer, in delivering the product or service, must be able to leverage the process in a cost-effective manner with a predictable financial return. The underlying cost-quality principle is this: for the producer, over the long term, high quality costs less than poor quality when the elegant process is in place for a given product or service.

Poor results are a consequence of poor processes, not of a poor workforce. While working in a factory, I oversaw a manufacturing operation of nearly two hundred people. One of my supervisors came to me one day with a report that an employee was apparently using an improper method of delivering material to the manufacturing line. It seems that instead of taking the tray of little tubes and dumping the tubes into the overhead chute, it was observed that she dumped the tubes into a small pan and then into the chute. This action resulted in an apparent extra step in the

17

process. Clearly, she had violated the standard procedure and the supervisor recommended we issue a citation. Keeping this principle in mind — *poor results are a consequence of poor processes, not of a poor workforce* — I made a trip to investigate the crime scene. I asked the young lady why she did it the "wrong" way instead of the "right" way as she had been instructed. She demonstrated the process to me. When she tried to dump the tray of tubes into the chute in the correct manner, several tubes missed the chute and fell to the floor. The tray holding the tubes was much larger than the mechanism receiving the tubes. Her solution was to dump the tray of tubes into a small, deep pan then dump the small pan of tubes into the chute. It was much easier to do this at waist level and then dump the pan into the overhead chute. Her "incorrect" method eliminated the potential to miss the chute when dumping the parts. I quickly recognized this young lady's action highlighted a very poor process. The failure was not in our workforce violating some carefully documented policy. On the contrary, the failure was in not proactively identifying the poor process and in continuing to reinforce the poorly designed process to our workforce. Subsequently, the process was changed. The new policy instituted the use of small pans rather than large trays to aid in the efficient handling of these parts. Had the worker been blamed and cited, the process would have never advanced and the workforce would have become disengaged. She would still be picking up tubes off the floor, *one by one*, wasting time and energy.

The relationship between cost and quality is traditionally viewed as proportional — the higher the quality of goods or services, the more expensive it must be to produce. However, this is not necessarily the case for a given product or service. The cost associated with producing something of value is sensitive to many inputs, but quality is a byproduct of the process employed to produce the good or service. Waste and inefficiency drive costs up much more than the mere pursuit of quality. Figure 2.1 demonstrates the traditional assumption of the dependency of quality on cost.

Figure 2.1 Traditional view of the cost-quality relationship

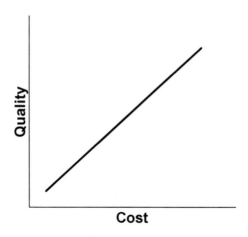

Cost and quality are not solely dependent on each other. Rather, both are a function of the robustness of process used to deliver the goods or services to the consumer. The traditional linear relationship may hold true when effective processes are not in place to ensure the desired outcome. However, a more complex relationship develops as processes are refined to support the quality and cost goals of the organization. Figure 2.2 gives a more complete view of the cost-quality relationship. Financial investment (cost) ceases to have a positive impact on quality at point B. Some companies may lose focus on quality in an effort to reduce cost once this perceived maximum quality level is reached. But it is at this point (B) that the quality can continue to increase as costs decrease. This is counter-intuitive to our traditional view of cost and quality. What causes this dramatic turn?

Figure 2.2 Progressive view of the cost-quality relationship

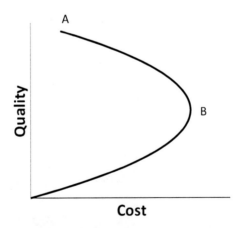

A DIFFERENT VIEW

The answer is the effective use of process to simultaneously improve quality and decrease costs. Resource investment is seldom the most practical means of improving quality. In fact, there is a point along the bottom half of the curve (Figure 2.2) in which businesses realize the diminishing returns of putting more and more financial resources into improving quality. The breakthrough comes upon the realization that quality is not a function of how much money is spent on the process. Quality and cost are much more dependent on the degree to which effective processes are used. When a process becomes so refined and efficient to the point of both increasing quality and decreasing cost, it has become elegant, as shown in Figure 2.3.

Figure 2.3 Three phases of the cost-quality relationship

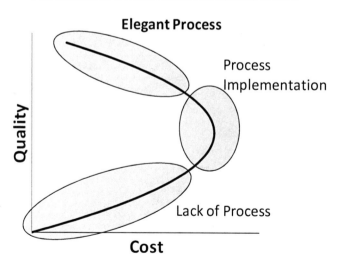

21

Figure 2.3 illustrates the three stages of the of process development in the cost-quality relationship. A linear relationship between cost and quality is typical of a delivery system that has a lack of process or process control. To some extent, additional resources can temporarily increase quality by adding tighter controls, supervision, inspection, or re-work loops. Once a business realizes the fallacy of dumping resources into a problem without addressing the root cause, it can enter the process implementation phase. In this phase, the pursuit of the elegant process allows a business to turn the corner on the cost-quality curve. The elegant process begins to emerge when quality increases and costs decrease at the same time.

Figure 2.3 Three phases of the cost-quality relationship

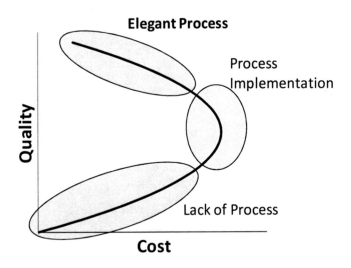

Complicated and cumbersome workflows generate high labor costs and suspect quality. The very essence of business is the continuous pursuit of customer satisfaction and the relentless struggle against rising costs. Some organizations are more successful in challenging the perceived proportional relationship between quality and cost. This relationship primarily exists as a mirage, viewing quality and cost-control as mutually exclusive, when, in fact, they can coexist. The common denominator of successful business ventures is the utilization of the elegant process as a means of simultaneously enhancing quality and reducing costs. The elegant process can be the difference in a profitable business and a business that closes its doors.

Chapter 3: The Intersection of Value, Cost, and Quality

"Quality is not an act. It is a habit."

-Aristotle

Quality and cost are inextricably linked to the level of process employed. Chaotic and confounded actions (the opposite of a process) produce high-cost and low-quality results. This is exemplified by lackluster service or defective products. When high-cost products and services are delivered at a higher cost than the consumer is willing to pay, the producer is left with a financial loss. Low-quality products are often priced far below fair market value to provide some hope of selling. Both situations are unattractive options to the producer. Prime organizations prevent both types of catastrophes by engaging in the use of elegant processes to control cost and promote quality. Quality and cost form the basis of the concept of value.

My wife and I decided to have new countertops installed in our kitchen. She had been looking for some time to replace the dated Formica countertops with something a little more upscale and durable. The local big box home improvement store happened to be running a great sale on solid surface countertops. We decided to purchase from the big box store over the smaller shops due to the big box's "satisfaction guaranteed" policy. We picked out the style and color she liked, placed the order and waited for the arrival of our new countertops, complete with a new kitchen sink. The big box store sub-contracted the job to an independent contractor located about an hour away. Three days later, a gentleman from the contractor came out to our house, measured the counters, and confirmed the order. The countertops and sink arrived a couple of weeks later. They were installed by the contractor without any issues. We soon noticed small rust spots developing along the curved metal partition separating the sink halves. I called the contractor who had installed the sink. He scheduled someone to come out to look at it "first thing in the morning." Reluctantly, I took time off work to meet the installer at the house. Of

THE INTERSECTION OF VALUE, COST, AND QUALITY

course, he arrived two hours later than scheduled. He looked at the sink, snapped several pictures and promised to call me in a couple of days.

A week went by — no phone call. By this time, the rust spots had turned into a line of rust. Upon close inspection, this line of rust was discovered to be a crack. I called the company and was greeted very kindly by a receptionist. My call was transferred to John. John informed me that the sink manufacturer reviewed the photos. The manufacturer's response to our claim declared "stainless steel doesn't rust." (Background information: I've spent my career working as an engineer, many of those years working with different types of stainless steel. True — some types of stainless steels don't rust. Some do. Rust is usually the result of a material defect such as contamination in the metal.)

I tried in vain to convince John that the defect was actually a crack in the metal highlighted by the rusting edge (and I know this because I am an engineer). Again, John reiterated that the manufacturer of the sink would not authorize his company to replace the sink, but I was welcome to call the manufacturer directly. Frustrated, my wife and I went directly to our local big box store and complained. Within a couple of days, John called us to set up an appointment for Bill to replace the sink — again first thing in the morning, again two hours late.

27

THE ELEGANT PROCESS

When Bill arrived on Thursday, he pounded and scraped and banged and clanked to get the old sink out. After working for some time, Bill was ready to set the new sink. As you might suspect, the sink he brought with him was the wrong style. Bill called back to the shop to talk to John. John could arrange to have the new sink installed "next week." I asked if they could install it today since this was now the fourth day I had taken off work to meet someone from his company at my house. John told me he just couldn't squeeze it in that day because the shop was an hour away and quitting time was fast approaching. But they could do it Saturday.

"Is that OK?" John asked.

"Not really, but OK," I said. I handed the phone to Bill. Bill and John talked for a few more minutes.

As Bill began to walk out of the house, he said "See you on Saturday around ten."

"Wait a second," I said. "Are you going to leave us here with no sink?" Bill grunted and reluctantly put the old sink back in. I am patient to a fault, but by this time I had had it! I went straight to the big box home improvement store where I purchased the countertops and sink. Sarah listened carefully to my sob story. To Sarah's credit, she called John directly and explained to him that the customer (me) needed to have this resolved today. To my surprise, John agreed for Bill to come back to my house at five in the afternoon with

28

THE INTERSECTION OF VALUE, COST, AND QUALITY

the correct sink. Not surprisingly, Bill arrived back at my house at seven with the correct sink. Within an hour, our sink was installed and Bill was on his way. After this very long and stressful ordeal, we are very satisfied with our new countertops and non-cracked stainless steel sink.

Sales and marketing may view this story as customer service failure. My manufacturing colleagues will cite this as a quality control issue. There are others who would characterize this as public relations disaster. All of these viewpoints may be accurate descriptions, but for better or worse, I view this as a *process failure*. In theory, the process of installing the countertops and sink was fairly simple, as shown below:

Step 1: Pick out countertops and sink.
Step 2: Pay for countertops and sink.
Step 3: Measure space for countertops.
Step 4: Make countertops.
Step 5: Install countertops and sink.

The simple five-step process very quickly turned into an eighteen-step process as summarized below:

Step 1: Pick out countertops and sink.
Step 2: Pay for countertops and sink.
Step 3: Measure space for countertops.
Step 4: Make countertops.
Step 5: Install countertops and sink.
Step 6: Return to worksite.
Step 7: Take pictures of sink.
Step 8: Send pictures of sink to manufacturer.
Step 9: Ignore customer.

29

Step 10: Deny responsibility.
Step 11: Get call from big box store to replace sink.
Step 12: Schedule return trip.
Step 13: Tear out cracked sink.
Step 14: Attempt to install wrong sink.
Step 15: Re-install cracked sink.
Step 16: Go back to shop and get new non-cracked sink.
Step 17: Tear out cracked sink again.
Step 18: Install new non-cracked sink.

This is a classic example of a process failure leading to customer dissatisfaction. As a result of this scenario, I was off work a total of fourteen additional hours to meet with and/or wait for Bill at my house. I, of course, had to take vacation time for these hours, which could have been cashed in later that year. In other words, Bill's process failure cost me real dollars. It cost John and Bill a satisfied customer and most likely a chain reaction of referrals that could have led to multiple jobs.

What happened to the contractor who installed the countertops is also significant. Because the sink manufacturer denied responsibility for the sink, the sub-contractor was stuck with the cost of replacing the sink. Let's consider a cost analysis of the project. The cost of the sink was two hundred dollars. The contractor made SIX trips to my house — double what the process required. Remember, their shop was an hour away, roughly sixty miles. The IRS reimbursement rate of fifty-five cents per mile roughly approximates the cost to drive a vehicle. Bill makes twenty dollars an hour and spent an hour at my house on each visit. John spent no less than two hours on the phone with me, Bill, Sarah, and the sink manufacturer. John makes twenty-five dollars an hour. Figure 3.1 shows a breakdown of the incremental cost of the incident absorbed by the contactor based on my analysis.

Figure 3.1: Cost of Quality Failure

Direct Labor:	3 hours x $20 per hour	$ 60
Admin Cost:	2 hours x $25 per hour	$ 50
Drive Time:	3 trips x 2 hours each x $20 per hour	$ 120
Vehicle Cost:	360 miles x $0.55 per mile	$ 198
Material Cost:	Replacement sink	+ $ 200
	Total cost of process failure	**$ 628**

My cost for the project was $3,368.91. Let's estimate the contractor's profit to be 8 percent after the big box home improvement store took its cut of the deal — leaving the contractor with $270 profit, assuming the job had been done right the first time. However, because of the process failure, the sub-contractor spent an additional $628 resulting in a $358 *loss* for the job ($270 – $628 = -$358).

Both the consumer and producer benefit when an elegant process fulfills the promise of bringing value to the customer under financially beneficial terms to the producer. In the event of a process failure, BOTH the consumer and the producer are negatively impacted and value is lost.

THE ELEGANT PROCESS

Value is created when the consumer (or customer) perceives a benefit relative to the time or money invested for that benefit. More simply,

$$\text{Value} = \frac{\text{Consumer's perception of benefit}}{\text{Consumer's investment of time or money}}$$

To the extent the producer can create the perception of consumer benefit at an acceptable level of investment on the part of the consumer, the producer has the opportunity to make a profit. (Profit is what is left over after the producer's costs are covered.) This book is not a how-to sales and marketing book nor is it about differentiating your product or service from others in your industry; rather, it is about how to build and design processes to prevent cost overruns, quality snafus, and customer dissatisfaction by utilizing well-designed processes. Providing the customer what he expects and when he expects it each and every time can be consistent with cost control and making a profit. Like marriage, it is cheaper to do it right the first time.

Axioms such as "you get what you pay for" and "quality doesn't come free" point to the consumer's expectation of having to pay a premium for exceptional quality in goods and services. Exceptional luxury is no doubt a differentiator in many business models. However, despite

32

the purchase price of any good or service, consumers expect some level of quality. In every transaction, there is the expectation of value in the mind of the consumer, regardless of the price paid.

I was standing in a customer service line at the local wholesale club. The woman in front of me was holding a jar half full of salsa. I was not exactly sure what was going on until it was her turn to speak with the man behind the customer service counter. She gave a long narrative about how she bought the salsa, took it home, tried it, and didn't like it though she clearly ate half the jar. To give you some perspective, she was a unique individual; so much so, I was not sure if her version of the salsa saga was a complaint or a joke. Though she didn't have a receipt, she demanded her money back. To my surprise and delight, the representative gave the lady a full refund, all of $5.79 — no questions asked.

To tell you the truth, I can't even imagine standing in a line for $5.79. But I learned a lesson. It was well worth the time spent standing in line. Despite how much or how little consumers pay for a product or service, there is always some expectation of quality. The Salsa Lady had an expectation of enjoying the salsa. Apparently, the salsa failed to meet her expectation despite the small amount of money she paid for it.

THE ELEGANT PROCESS

In my infamous countertop experience, I did receive the benefit of beautiful and, perhaps more importantly, wife-pleasing countertops. However, my unforeseen investment in time and hassle in getting the sink replaced diminished my valuation of the entire exchange. Similarly, the contractor's increased cost related to my dissatisfaction turned his expected profit into an unexpected loss. Had the contractor had processes in place to prevent this quality failure, he would have turned a profit on this project. The process was not elegant and therefore lacks the long-term ability to sustain a profit.

Quality and cost are not two sides of the same coin as some may suggest. It is not an either-or proposition. The words *quality* and *cost* describe the output and input of a given series of deliberate events. *Quality* describes the output of a process relative to the benefit it creates in the mind of the consumer. *Cost* is the sum total of the producer's investment in the process. Thus, cost and quality are the relative perspectives from which both the consumer and producer view the same series of events. Because cost and quality are just different views of the same process, they can simultaneously exist to the benefit of both the producer AND consumer. Enhancing quality and reducing costs requires correctly designing and executing the process to optimize the benefit to both parties involved in the exchange.

Chapter 4: Adding Value

"Waste is the enemy of value."

One evening on my way home from work, I remembered that I needed to pick up a few items from the grocery store. There are two grocery stores close to my home: the low-cost chain grocery store and the higher-cost "market" grocery store. The pricier store requires a left-hand turn across a busy street, while the less expensive store is a block closer and does not require crossing a busy street. I chose to go to the low-cost chain store; closer, cheaper — easy decision, right? I found what I needed and went up to the checkout line to pay. There was only one teenaged employee helping customers, and unfortunately, self-checkout lanes were not an option at this store. So I had no choice but to wait in a line of five or six people, some of whom were there to do their entire week's worth of grocery shopping. I thought to myself as I patiently waited, *Next time, go to the other store.* A week later, I found myself needing to go back to the grocery store to pick up a couple of things for my wife. Remembering, but ignoring, my previous experience, I wheeled once again into the lower-priced, more accessible grocery store. I picked up the few items that I needed, and again I waited to pay for the groceries, this time a little less patiently. I thought again to myself as I waited, *Next time, go to the other store.* I now faithfully shop at the higher-end grocery store every single time. Why? The lower cost and more accessible store wastes my time, totally counteracting the benefits of being closer and cheaper. Waste is the enemy of value.

In Chapter 3, we discussed the concept of value, that is, what benefits the customer. Creating value for the consumer must be cascaded throughout all of the producer's processes. By definition, a value-adding step transforms the product or service in a way that is beneficial to the consumer.

A couple of years ago, I bought a pre-owned Toyota pickup truck from an auto wholesaler. In order to obtain license plates, I had to go to the local Department of Motor Vehicles. (Before I go into the analysis of my experience, I will first say that contrary to what you might expect, the entire experience was pretty good. The wait time was manageable and the competency and friendliness of the staff was great.) As is typical for me, I viewed my entire experience as a process, thus in need of a thorough analysis.

I walked into the DMV and stood in a short line at the greeter's station. The greeter handed me a clipboard with a form to fill out. I promptly filled out the form and returned it. I was given a number and asked to have a seat. Within a few minutes when my number was called, I approached the counter and handed the young lady my number. She apologized and informed me I had been directed to the wrong counter, and that I needed to walk two spaces to the left. The customer service representative there helped me, and I walked away with my new license plates.

To analyze this process properly, I first have to identify why I went to the DMV. What was the value generating proposition for which I was paying? What was the benefit I received because of my visit to the DMV? What could the DMV offer me that no other organization could? It was the opportunity to obtain license plates. I was not paying to stand in line, to fill out a form, to wait for my number to be called, nor to walk to the wrong counter. I was only paying for license plates.

This experience demonstrates the four types of process steps within the realm of process design: value-adding, supporting, avoidable, and abnormal. Let's define each of these types of process steps and relate them back to my DMV experience.

Value-adding process step: a step in the process that brings a benefit to the customer and for which the customer is willing to pay.

Supporting process step: a step in the process that does not bring a direct benefit to the customer but is necessary in order to bring the benefit to the customer.

Avoidable process step: a step in the process that does not benefit the customer and is not necessary in bringing a benefit to the customer.

Abnormal process step: a counter-productive and unexpected event in the process that inconveniences the customer. Or, more simply, a *mistake.*

Supporting, avoidable, and abnormal process steps are considered *waste. Waste* is any activity that does not bring direct value or benefit to the consumer. While the supporting

ADDING VALUE

process steps are *necessary* and cannot be eliminated, they are nonetheless considered *waste*. All waste is the enemy of value. Waste decreases the value of the process from the perspective of either the consumer or producer. In my coaching and training sessions, I get pushback on the idea that a step can be necessary, but also wasteful. "How can it be a waste if it is absolutely necessary?" I am often asked. My response is this: *waste* and *value-add* are technical terms, having very specific meanings in the context of process design. It is the nomenclature used to distinguish what the customer is willing to pay for (*value*) and what he or she is not (*waste*).

To reduce this angst over the term *waste*, we distinguish between *supporting* and *avoidable* process steps. If the step is supporting the value stream and is necessary, so be it. Nevertheless, the consumer does not want to pay extra for it. An example in a restaurant setting of a supporting process step is transportation. When we go out to a restaurant to eat, the benefit is the enjoyment of a good meal that we do not have to prepare or clean up after. That is what we pay for. We are not paying for the transportation required to get the food from the farm to our table. We assume all the transportation costs associated with moving the food from the farm to the vendor, from the vendor to the pantry, from the pantry to the kitchen, and from the kitchen to the table are contained within the price of the meal. Can you imagine your surprise if you were charged a delivery fee for your meal in addition to the cost of the meal?

If the consumer is not willing to pay for the process step as a standalone product or service, it is considered a non-value-adding (wasteful) process step. True, the food must be transported from the farm to our table. There is no escaping this supporting process step. But, it would also be ridiculous for us to order a meal and receive separate checks — one for the food and one for the transportation. Despite the necessity of transportation, it is not what precipitates the financial exchange between the consumer (those of us eating) and the producer (the restaurant).

Each category of process step requires a different response. A value-adding process step should flow to the consumer, creating the benefit expeditiously. If the process steps are supporting the value-adding activities and cannot be eliminated altogether, they should be reduced or compressed as much as possible. It is always desirable to reduce, decrease, or eliminate tasks that add time but do not benefit the overall value to the consumer. Discarding completely the avoidable activities serves the best interests of both the consumer (by reducing wait time) and the producer (by reducing cost). Similarly, the abnormal process steps (accidents, mistakes, unplanned events) must also be eliminated as they are inconvenient and counter-beneficial to the consumer. These abnormalities are somewhat more difficult to eliminate as they are not intentional acts of failure, but represent an uncontrolled process. The figure below simplifies the hierarchy of value-adding and non-value-adding process steps in graphical form.

Figure 4.1 Value and Non-Value-Adding Process Steps

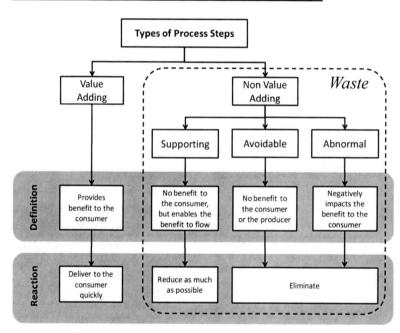

Referring back to my DMV experience, we can analyze the process and determine to which of the four categories each step belongs. To analyze the process of obtaining license plates properly, begin by sketching a process map of the experience as shown in Figure 4.2.

41

Figure 4.2 "Purchase License Plate at the DMV" Process Map

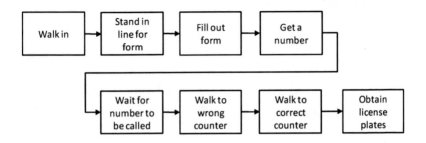

We can now more easily analyze each action and determine in which category the process step fits. Using the process map as a baseline, the process steps can be converted into tabular form noting the action, type of activity, and explanation in Figure 4.3.

Figure 4.3 Process Analysis of DMV Experience

Action	Type of Activity	Explanation
Walk in	Supporting	Facilitates the initiating of the process
Stand in line for form	Avoidable	Waiting is almost always avoidable
Fill out form	Supporting	Required to facilitate the value-adding step
Get a number	Avoidable	Has no direct influence on the value-adding step
Wait for number to be called	Avoidable	Waiting is almost always avoidable
Walk to wrong counter	Abnormal	Not intended part of the process; a mistake
Walk to correct counter	Supporting	Necessary to advance the process
Obtain license plates	Value Adding	The benefit to the consumer

Some might argue that with the online service capabilities of the DMV, *walking in* becomes an avoidable process step. However, in the context of this process, which is *to **go** to the DMV to obtain license plates*, one must, by definition, **go** to the DMV. Recognizing that *walking in* is a supporting process step signifies the potential to reduce the consumer's effort, but not totally eliminate it. To say that *walking in* is avoidable (not necessary) changes the nature of the process and adds a significant element of technology to the equation.

A second point to consider is waiting time. In general, waiting is almost always considered waste. If I were the only person in the DMV or there were more customer service representatives than customers, I would not have to wait. Therefore, making me wait is a conscious (and financial) decision made by the DMV management. But the waiting itself is not a legal prerequisite of obtaining license plates. There is no regulation, condition, or universal law requiring one to wait in line as a pre-condition for obtaining license plates.

Contrast waiting in line at the DMV with the waiting required to produce whiskey. In order for the whiskey to develop its unique properties and taste, there is a necessary benefit in allowing the whiskey to "wait" (ferment) in barrels for a period of time. In this case, the "waiting" is considered

43

to add value because it enhances or improves the condition of the whiskey. This waiting is what makes whiskey, whiskey. However, my waiting in line at the DMV does not enhance the value of the license plates.

My walking up to the wrong counter brings us to the third point. This process step is *abnormal*. It was a mistake and, ideally, it should not have happened. A robust or elegant process would have eliminated the possibility of this happening. It is considered abnormal waste because it mistakenly added time to the process without promoting value. In order to reduce waste and increase value, we must seek to eliminate these types of abnormal activities.

To reiterate, the terms discussed in this chapter (*waste, value-adding, supporting, avoidable, and abnormal process steps*) are technical terms and apply very specifically to analyzing processes. Do not interpret this to mean that people who perform non-value-adding tasks are not necessary. Analysis must be done on the process itself, and not the people, to determine how best to reduce or eliminate all wasteful activity. This topic is more fully addressed in Chapter 13. All processes and process steps contain elements of non-value-adding activity. The goal is to advance our process to a more elegant design by eliminating waste where possible and significantly reducing it when eliminating it is not an option.

Chapter 5: The Seven Wastes

---

*"He that idly loses five shilling worth of time,
loses five shilling, and might as prudently
throw five shilling into the river."*

-Benjamin Franklin

In 1995, the movie *Seven* was released, starring Morgan Freeman, Brad Pitt, and Kevin Spacey. *Seven* chronicles the events of a retiring detective (Freeman) and his protégé (Pitt) investigating a series of twisted crimes based loosely on the seven deadly sins. The crime scenes each contain clues as to the whereabouts of the psychopathic killer (Spacey). Process design contains its own version of the seven deadly sins, except they are called the seven wastes.

THE ELEGANT PROCESS

(Fortunately, the only commonalities between the seven deadly sins and the seven process wastes is that there are seven and they are all bad.) In this chapter, we will investigate the seven wastes of process design. These wastes are often represented by the acronym TIM WOOD. TIM WOOD stands for Transportation, Inventory, Motion, Waiting, Over-production, Over-processing and Defects.

Transportation waste is a non-value-adding event involving the movement of materials, supplies, people, or services in a way that does not directly enhance the benefit of the goods or services being provided. Transporting requires significant time and cost — time and cost for which the consumer is generally not willing to pay. Because the consumer is not willing to pay for it, transportation is often the expense of the producer. In the previous chapter, we discussed the transportation required to bring food to the table of a restaurant. We called this transportation non-value-adding work, but decided some transportation was still necessary. By terming transportation *waste*, elegant process design implores us to reduce or eliminate transportation as much as possible. Dell Computer recognized this type of waste and implemented a transportation reduction strategy at its Flat Rock, Texas, facility. Dell's strategy was to have its vendors set up supply depots or warehouses in close proximity to the factory. It was up to the vendors to keep the

46

THE SEVEN WASTES

warehouses stocked with components used in the manufacture of computers. This "just in time" inventory resulted in cost and time reduction in delivering material to the factory. In part, this enabled Dell to build computers on-demand, just days after the computer was ordered.

Inventory is a sign of waste. Outlet shopping malls dot the American landscape. They are filled with the excess inventory from factories and retail department stores. In the ideal scenario, your favorite brand name producer would make only the exact pieces and quantity of clothing it could sell at a retail price and eliminate the need for outlet malls. If the producer produced too many sweaters, for example, it would have to sell the excess sweaters at a discounted price in order to reduce the potential for a financial loss. (This is Economics 101!) However, if the producer produces too few sweaters, there will be a sweater shortage, which will result in lost revenue. It is this fear of lost revenue combined with a calculated risk which encourages a producer to produce more sweaters than it can sell at a retail price. So, why is this waste? Eventually, won't all the sweaters sell? Maybe. But that is not the point. The producer recognizes there is no way to accurately predict exactly how many sweaters to produce. Excess inventory is a hedge against the risk of selling out — *a hedge for which the consumer cares nothing about.* Inventory is precisely waste because the excess sweaters

47

represent both time and money being frozen in the hand of and at the expense of the producer. The consumer is not willing to pay for the cost associated with storing and maintaining excess inventory and really does not care if the inventory exists. Simply put, excess inventory is a symptom of unmanaged process risk. Therefore, inventory becomes a necessary waste, but one that should be minimized. The solution is to design processes to minimize the risk of producing excess inventory.

Motion is the waste associated with human energy being unnecessarily expended in the workplace. While transportation involves the movement of "stuff," motion pertains to the movement of people and machines. Transportation is measured in miles and hours, but motion is typically measured in feet or inches and minutes or seconds. Obviously, without motion, nothing happens. Therefore, motion may be necessary to complete the process. But unnecessary motion must be reduced if not eliminated altogether.

One evening while riding my bicycle, I noticed my left pedal was loose. I hopped off the bike to check it out. I found the crank arm (the rod that connects the pedal to the crank) was slipping slightly, but not too badly. I continued to ride for a couple of days. As the slipping grew worse, I became concerned because the slippage made it difficult to stay upright as my left-leg peddling tried to keep pace with my right-leg peddling. This extra motion was from my left leg constantly having to compensate for the slipping part. Finally, I decided I was tired of this extraneous peddling and headed to the bike shop to buy a replacement part. I installed the new crank arm and began to ride. It struck me how smooth and efficient my peddling stroke had become. My balance was sturdier, and the ride was much smoother. Because I analyze the events of my life out of pure habit, I began to consider what it was about this malfunction that caused such a disturbance to my peddling process. The answer: wasted motion. I expended a tremendous amount of wasted energy trying to compensate for a broken process.

Waiting, delays, and idle time are all sources of waste. When was the last time you were in an airport? Did you find any benefit to waiting, hanging out in the terminal, wondering when or if your flight would ever leave? Of course not. Process design is no different. Waiting is the absence of any value-adding motion. It is often caused by an imbalance between supply and demand, stalling either the consumer's or producer's process. When work is batched improperly or processes are not properly balanced, workflows stop and start like New York traffic. Constant and erratic pauses within the process waste the most valuable resource of all: time. And time is money. From the producer's vantage point, wasting time means wasting money and losing profit. Waiting on a product or service decreases the benefit of that product or service in the mind of the consumer. An elegant process is one in which waiting and delays are eliminated.

Over-production is the cause of excess inventory. Over-production occurs when demand is overestimated and too much product is made or too much service is provided. While *inventory* waste is the misuse of assets, over-production is the waste commonly associated with excess labor, machine use, or raw material consumption. The infamous TPM Reports, made so by the movie *Office Space*, were reports generated in great quantity and contained little or no useful information. Companies tend to generate newsletters, reports, and other communications for wide-scale distribution without regard to the cost of managing the mountain of paper. Ideally, such communiqué should be produced on-demand, or *as needed, when needed,* to prevent over-production waste.

Over-processing is time and effort spent handling the same work piece over and over again. Over-processing screams of forms and data handling. Businesses often assume it is cheaper and more efficient to pass paperwork along progressively to lower-wage employees. Lost in this assumption is the cost implication of moving the paper from one workstation to another. The time, both in the passing of the paper and in the stacking of paper, is not always considered. Take, for example, a simple invoice. An invoice arrives at the office via post and is received by an office assistant. The assistant opens the envelope and places the invoice in a stack with a dozen others, awaiting the move to the accounts payable department. The interoffice courier comes around once or twice a day to pick up the invoices and hands them off to the accounts payable office. A clerk handles the invoices, sorts and stacks according to approver, and forwards them to the approvers. Eventually, the approvers approve the invoice for payment and may or may not send the invoice back to accounts payable for processing. Invoices received by the accounts payable office are verified for a signature, matched to the original order, and entered into the accounting software. Then, the funds are released. Though we like to delay payment for as long as possible, a tremendous amount of cost accumulates with each handling and re-handling of the same invoice. Additional failure opportunities are created as invoices can be routed incorrectly, lost, and become delinquent. All these inefficiencies are the result of non-value-adding activity in the form of over-processing. Each time an invoice is handled, stacked, or transported, time resources are squandered.

Defects are the final category of waste. A defect is the result of mistakes, failures, flaws, and inadequacies in the outcome of the process. Defects lead to one or both of two possibilities. The first possibility is a do-over. I remember as a kid playing the game of 500 (a game played with a baseball and bat in the street) with the other kids in the neighborhood. Inevitably, one kid would call a "do-over," an opportunity to hit the ball again without losing any points. Do-overs in the business world, however, are not without consequence. They represent real cost in recovering or reproducing the product or service without a defect.

The second result of a defect is loss of customer satisfaction. This occurs when the service recovery or product replacement is not sufficient to reshape the value judgment of the consumer. The first consequence, a do-over, costs money, time, and effort, and will have an immediate and quantifiable repercussion on the part of the producer. However, the second result, an unhappy consumer, is not immediately known or quantifiable, but could very well represent the greater loss.

Effective process design must address defect potential, preferably in the prevention of defects altogether. Complete prevention of defects is not often possible or financially justifiable. In those cases, recovery or risk mitigation may prove to be viable options within the process design.

The existence of the TIM WOOD wastes highlights opportunities to improve processes. Again, waste cannot always be eliminated; however, each instance of waste should trigger a warning light in our minds of possible opportunities to improve, streamline, compress, or redesign steps within our processes. Constantly challenging ourselves, "Is this the best it can get?" is a key driver in designing the elegant process. Our ever-evolving business environment coupled with new and exciting technology offers ample opportunity to improve our operational processes with the explicit goal of enhancing quality and reducing costs.

Chapter 6: Build the Process

"Beauty is profundity wrapped in simplicity."

L et's conduct a theoretical experiment. Suppose I were to come into your business and ask a receptionist, "What is your company's process for ensuring all employees have successfully completed customer service training?" What would her response be? Typically, I would get one of two responses. The first possible and preferable response would be for the receptionist to describe her own experience of how the company explained the

THE ELEGANT PROCESS

critical role of customer service in the interview process. Your employee might go on to tell me about a class or mentoring program that emphasized customer service. She could talk about how your organization measures customer service and solicits feedback from the customer base. To close the loop, customer feedback would be used to enhance yearly training programs.

The second possible and more likely response would be the receptionist fumbling over words, trying to communicate a series of random past experiences into some sort of coherent conversation. The explanation would contain an almost infinite number of "ifs" and "ums" followed by "sometimes," "except when," "sort of" and "maybe-kinda." Getting this type of answer leads me to suspect there is no real process for customer service training.

When I start on a new project or begin work in a new department, I always ask the team to describe their workflow or process. Without fail, I get a response similar to either one of the aforementioned. Based on which of these responses I get, I immediately know whether we will be designing and building the process from scratch or if we will be improving the existing process. Designing or redesigning a process follows the same basic principles. Here, I will deal specifically with designing the process and how to build it from the ground up.

Start with the end in mind. What is your vision? What do you want the process to produce? Remember, we defined a process as a series of actions leading to the accomplishment of a goal. So the first question for the process designer is, "What is the goal for this process?" Knowing your end game up front will keep you and your team focused on delivering an elegant process.

Asking this question early on may seem overly simple and elementary. Who would design a process without knowing what the objective is? The answer is a little more subtle. You might know what the objective is. You may also assume your team knows exactly what the process must accomplish. But let's assume our employees do not always think in big-picture terms. They may perceive that the goal of the process is merely to accomplish a series of tasks. However, they may not realize that the goal is to generate value.

Take as an example designing a process to bring in job applicants for the purpose of screening or hiring them for employment. Your team may view this as simply a hiring process and assume your goal merely to hire more employees. However, the actual big-picture objective is to attract and retain the right people, with the right skill set and attitude. If your objective is just to hire people, your process would look much different than if your objective is to hire qualified applicants to fulfill your company's labor needs.

Sketch a high-level process map. The *process map* communicates the shape and major direction of the process. It is not necessary at this point to define *how* to accomplish the individual tasks, only to show that we *must* accomplish the individual tasks. Our goal is to match qualified applicants to our company's needs and hire them; thus, our process map should include these elements. Our first draft of the process map might look like Figure 6.1 below:

Figure 6.1 Basic Process Elements (Beginning, Midpoint, End)

Before you think this too easy, it is merely the first step in developing a basic high-level process map. From a pragmatic standpoint, there is a BIG gap between "Determine company's needs" and "Receive applications" and "Hire qualified candidate." Even for a high-level process map, we need more information.

Let's begin with the gap between the first two boxes. What must happen after we determine our company's needs but before we find qualified applicants? There are a few things: we must convert our company's needs into a job description; we must advertise the job description; and we must receive applications. When we add these steps into our high-level process map, we are left with a partial process map shown in Figure 6.2.

Figure 6.2 Major Tasks or Sub-Processes

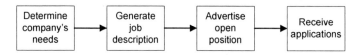

Now we follow the same logic to fill in the major gaps between "Receive application" and "Hire qualified candidate." Depending on your hiring policies, you might want to add steps such as screen qualified applicants, interview screened applicants, and conduct reference checks on candidates. The result would be a process map as shown in Figure 6.3.

Figure 6.3 Complete Process Map

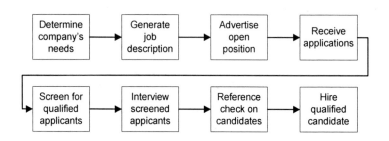

THE ELEGANT PROCESS

Notice this process map does not describe in detail any of the individual process tasks. This is entirely intentional. The high-level process map's purpose is twofold. First, define the "goal posts" of the process. *Goal posts* describe the process boundaries and highlight the primary focus of the design effort. Anything before or after what appears on the process map is not germane to the process we are building. Those topics belong in another process map altogether. The second purpose of the process map is to define the steps within the process to be addressed as sub-processes or tasks. The extent to which these sub-processes or tasks flow from one to the other will determine the overall efficiency of the larger process.

Each of the boxes in our hiring process map can be further broken down into a series of enumerated list of tasks. For example, the first box entitled "Determine company's needs" could be elaborated upon to include a series of procedures necessary to initiate the job requisition, such as a financial justification, required approvals, and the education or skill-level requirements.

A complete process can be developed using the process map as a guideline. The following gives significant detail to the process map, filling in the individual tasks required to complete the process. Figure 6.4 outlines this process as a numbered list of tasks.

60

BUILD THE PROCESS

Figure 6.4 Detailed Process Flow

Determine company's need: Hiring Manager
1. Conduct work flow analysis
2. Decide hours per pay period
3. Financial justification
4. Submit requisition for approval
5. Obtain approval

Generate job description: Hiring Manager
6. Define qualifications
7. Determine required education
8. Verify consistency with other positions
9. Assign pay range

Advertise open position: Human Resource Specialist
10. Post to online job board
11. Notify external recruiters

Receive applications: Human Resource Specialist
12. Receive inquiries via email or US post
13. Enter information into database
14. Sort and forward to HR manager

Screen for qualified applicants: Human Resource Manager
15. Separate qualified and unqualified applicants
16. Arrange phone screens
17. Conduct phone screens
18. Compile phone screen results
19. Forward results to hiring manager

Interview screened applicants: Hiring Manager
20. Select top candidates
21. Schedule interviews
22. Arrange travel
23. Finalize application
24. Conduct interview
25. Select preliminary candidates

Reference check on candidates: Human Resource Specialist
26. Verify references
27. Validate work history
28. Background/criminal history check
29. Drug screen

Hire qualified candidate: Human Resource Manager
30. Extend offer
31. Negotiate compensation
32. Set start date

61

Contrast the process map shown in Figure 6.3 with the detailed process flow in Figure 6.4. The process map defines the scope, not necessarily the tasks of the process as shown in Figure 6.4. The process map is intended only to identify the starting point of the process, the desired outcome, and the major milestones along the way. Think of this map as the process framework, defining the structure, critical path, and sequencing essential to achieving its purpose. Additional details can be added to produce a more detailed view once all of the nuances of the process are understood. The objective of building the process map is to gain a clear understanding of the current state of the process as it actually is or as it is assumed to be. The foundation of the elegant process is a clear determination of the *"what"* and the *"when,"* not so much the *"who"* and the *"how."* Trying to devise a process by initially fretting with the *"who"* and *"how"* detracts from the systematic development of a robust and elegant process.

The process map is the fundamental first step in engineering the elegant process. It communicates the current state or general direction of the target process at a macro level rather than provides details. At any point in designing the process, the process map can be used as a springboard for other process presentations such as flow charts or diagrams. Rather than documenting the process minutia, the high-level map allows us to overlook the details intentionally in order to focus on the value-generating aspects of the process. The following chapters utilize this focus on value to streamline and optimize process performance from a quality and cost perspective.

Chapter 7: Shrink the Process

"I would have written a shorter letter,
but I did not have the time."

−Blaise Pascal

ack in kindergarten, too many years ago to admit, I recall a game we played to teach against the ills of gossip. Our class of 20 five-year-olds sat in a circle. The teacher whispered in the first student's ear a simple phrase, "Jack and Jill went up the hill to fetch a pail of water." The first student whispered the phrase in the second student's ear and could do so only once. The second student repeated what he heard into the ear of the third student. And the phrase was passed from child to child, until the final child blurted out, "There's no water in the potty!"

Recently, my daughter came home from school having played the game in her fifth grade class. The phrase began as, "The northeastern storm has caused an early dismissal," and was intended to alert the students of a severe storm moving in, and they would be getting out of school early that day. The phrase morphed conveniently into, "There will be no homework tonight!" Certainly, we could all cite examples of either grade school games or workplace information being passed along, growing, changing and ultimately misrepresenting the original intent of the conversation. This deviation from perfect can be quantified and is communicated as the process *yield*. *Yield* is a measure of a process's ability to produce a pure result. If a process has a yield of 80%, it produced only 80% of its expected outcome correctly. This yield calculation can be used to describe a process's state relative to output, quality, efficiency, or effectiveness — any one of many process metrics.

There is direct correlation between the concept of yield and quality regardless of how quality may be defined in your organization. Quality is a measure of how well or how often your business satisfies its customers. Quantifiably, it is a measure of good products available compared to total population of all products. Qualitatively, it is a scored measure of customers' perceptions of services rendered. In either case, this principle holds true — the more complicated the process or the more process steps required, the more opportunities exist for errors, mistakes, and failures. If errors represent a loss of customer satisfaction, then reducing errors will produce higher customer satisfaction. Defects resulting from process errors can be dramatically reduced if the opportunity for making those mistakes is reduced. Basically, *simpler processes tend to produce better results.*

In the case of the gossip game, the yield is a measure of the accuracy of the statement as it is passed along the series of children. If the first child communicates to the second child a phrase that is 90% accurate, the entire process henceforth cannot be more than 90% accurate from the second child forward (assuming the teacher does not intervene). The second child then begins with a 90% accurate phrase and communicates it to the third child in a manner only 90% accurate. The third child now hears a phrase that is 90% of 90%, or 81% accurate. Following this logic, the total accuracy of the entire process then depends on two things: the accuracy of the transmission at each step and the total number of transmissions. The yield of the process step is calculated by multiplying the incoming accuracy by the transmission accuracy. This calculation is repeated for each process step using the incoming and outgoing accuracy rates. In our model above, our process yield for 20 students each transmitting the phrase with 90% accuracy would produce a total process yield of about 12%. Illustrated graphically, the process degradation is represented as such:

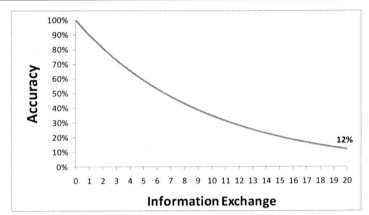

Figure 7.1 Accuracy of a phrase passed along by 20 children

If we relate the concept of yield back to our discussion of waste, the 12% yield represents the residual value left at the end of the process. The 88% (100%–12%) lost during the course of the process is waste. In this case, waste takes on the form of defects. Notice how the compounding effect of 90% quickly produces a much lower overall process yield.

One might be tempted to assume 90% to be fairly accurate and desirable. But as evidenced by our gossip illustration, a 90% yield, especially when compounded, is not always desirable. However, the threshold for accuracy depends also on the context of what is being measured. You

SHRINK THE PROCESS

would not be pleased if the electricity running to your home or business was 90% reliable. If that were the case, your home or office would be without power for 2.4 hours or 144 minutes each day — quite an inconvenience in the modern world! In fact, in today's fast-paced work environment, 2.4 hours without Internet or mobile connectivity would send most of us into a tailspin. On the other hand, a pro-basketball player who consistently hit 90% of his shots could name his own salary! Each process within each business within an industry has its own expectation of process yield. Yet, the mathematic principle behind this concept holds true in all cases and forms a measurement method by which to gage overall process effectiveness.

The pursuit of a more elegant process requires two distinct actions with regard to accuracy. First, every opportunity to reduce the number of process steps must be taken. Whether the process involves property management or a supply chain, manufacturing or accounting, the simpler the process, the less likely errors will occur. This is not a new concept. Paraphrasing Ockham's razor from the fourteenth century, "The simplest solution is often the best solution." By merely reducing the number of steps or tasks within a process, the yield will significantly increase. What would happen if we reduced the number of children in our circle from twenty to ten? Our overall gossip chain accuracy would

69

increase from 12% to 35%. If we could further reduce the process to just five steps, we could see an accuracy approaching 60%.

Figure 7.2 Accuracy of a phrase passed along 20 children

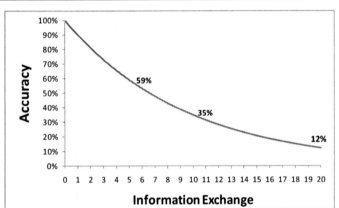

It may seem impossible to imagine a scenario in your business environment with an opportunity to reduce the number of process steps from twenty to five. However, I have found that there are almost always opportunities to shrink the process. I would challenge you to look at each process step in light of the value it creates. Are there opportunities to simplify steps, combine functions, or eliminate tasks altogether?

I was put in charge of a project to reduce the number of times paper files were handled. Many people needed access to these files for reporting, tracking, and quality assurance purposes. The team and I conducted an analysis on how many people accessed the files, when they accessed the files, and how long it took them to finalize their work. As it turned out, an individual file was touched about eight times sequentially over a three-month period before all the necessary information was gathered. At first, the team thought it was impossible to reduce the number of times this information was examined. Each person who touched the file had a very important and specialized job to do. The lingering question was whether or not the team could re-shuffle duties, cross-train and minimize the total number of times the information was handled.

The contents of those files contained time-sensitive information. Waiting three months or more to consolidate all the information led to a delay in important decisions being made. The team worked diligently and intelligently following the steps outlined in the introduction of this book. Within two weeks, a process requiring only two touches was developed. This new process was instituted and became fully operational over the next two months.

This reduction in the number of process steps also decreased the total process time of each file from three months to three days. Management now had the information it needed real-time rather than waiting until the information was almost outdated to make strategic decisions.

Financially, shrinking the process made sense as well. Each time the files passed from one person to the next, waste was generated in the form of transportation, over-processing, and waiting. For each of those wastes, there was a direct correlation to dollars spent; and dollars spent unnecessarily, I might add.

Suppose the cost to the company each time the file was handled was five dollars in labor costs. It may not seem like such a big deal to reduce handling costs from forty dollars (eight touches times five dollars per touch) to ten dollars (two touches times five dollars per touch) for a net reduction of thirty dollars per file. But consider the impact if ten thousand files per year needed to be analyzed. The improvement project would yield a total cost savings of $300,000 per year, due entirely to reducing the number of steps in the process.

The second element of improving total process yield is increasing the yield of each individual step or task. This is a methodology unto itself and is typically much more difficult to do. Optimizing individual process steps requires a more rigorous and disciplined method of improvement. Rather than viewing processes as a series of sub-processes or tasks as we have in this book, more advanced improvement tools require examining the process as a function of its inputs and outputs. Looking at a process in this way allows us to understand the critical levers of a process (its inputs); and by tightly controlling the inputs, we can predict and produce the desired output. This level of process analysis falls outside the intent and scope of this book and is best utilized only after the principles outlined in this book are successfully applied.

Overly complex processes result in poor quality outcomes and are often very expensive to maintain. Each movement or task within a process presents risk to the outcome of the process. The higher the total risk contained in the process, the more likely a failure will occur and the desired result will not be achieved or cost target met. Therefore, it is of utmost importance to reduce or combine tasks in an effort to shrink the process into its most compact, risk-averse, and cost-efficient form.

Chapter 8: Get Rhythm, Part 1 - Tempo

"Yes, a jumpy rhythm makes you feel so fine;
It'll shake all the troubles from your worried mind."

-Johnny Cash

Ensuring an elegant process requires an understanding of and appreciation for *process rhythm*. *Process rhythm* is the flow and cadence at which the process moves in time. We tend to think of rhythm as it relates to music or a beating heart or your favorite poem. Processes also have rhythms. Process rhythm defines how each step in the process works together to create a continuous, synchronous process flow. I remember going to

75

THE ELEGANT PROCESS

Philadelphia one year to watch the Dallas Cowboys play the Philadelphia Eagles back in the Troy Aikman / Emmett Smith / Michael Irvin era. It was the first professional football game I had ever attended in person. As I watched the Dallas offense, I was amazed by the precision and timing of all eleven players. One play in particular sticks in my mind. The ball was snapped, the offensive line battled the defenders, and the wide receivers took off down the field, running their routes. Aikman let the ball fly. I was not sure who he was throwing it to! Just after he released the ball, Michael Irvin cut back inside toward the middle of the field. Michael reached out and caught the ball without breaking stride. Immediately, he was surrounded and brought down by the Eagles' defense.

The reason I remember this so vividly is not because of the beer being tossed in the air. It was not the Eagle fans screaming and cursing. It was sheer elegance of how the quarterback, receiver, and offensive line worked in perfect concert to pull off such a play. Surrounded by passionate Eagle fans, I kept these observations of the Cowboys' perfect rhythm to myself, of course. I've watched football on TV for as long as I can remember. But watching professional football on television never gave me an appreciation for the process rhythm required to complete a thirty-yard pass. It was not

76

until that point that I understood just how important rhythm is to football.

And the same is true for process. It takes many pieces working together at the same time, for the same reason, in the same rhythm. Without a rhythm, a process can quickly disintegrate into random actions, each marching to the beat of its own drum. Rhythm is the unifying force holding together all the tasks and actions contained within a process. This rhythmic force has two central components: tempo and synchronicity.

Tempo characterizes the periodic nature of the rhythm. Or, more simply, how fast the process is moving. We can say it takes an average 3.4 minutes to resolve a customer service complaint over the phone. An invoice may take seventy-two hours to process. A bag of popcorn can be popped in a microwave in two minutes. Process time defines the tempo of a process and is typically measured in time units or number of cycles per time unit.

The tempo of a process must match the rate of consumer demand in order to reduce or eliminate waste. When process tempo does not exactly match consumer demand, one of two types of waste occurs. Process tempo exceeding the rate of customer demand (process moving faster than the consumer can consume) causes the waste of over-production and likely results in excess inventory.

THE ELEGANT PROCESS

Consider, for a moment, a quick-service restaurant. What happens when burgers are cooked and assembled at a rate higher than that of customers entering the restaurant? Too many burgers are made and are at risk of not being sold or customers returning them for being cold or stale. The second risk is if the producer's process moves much slower than the consumer's demand requires. If consumers are coming in faster than the burgers can be cooked and packaged, the customers will be left waiting, which is also waste. Some customers will choose to wait in line; others will choose to leave. Obviously, the goal is to match production tempo to consumer demand in order to minimize over-production risk while keeping wait times as short as possible.

Contrasting iTunes with FYE illustrates the concept of demand-triggered process. FYE is an entertainment retail store, specializing in the sale of CDs and DVDs, while iTunes is an online catalog of downloadable music, games, movies, and books. Both FYE and iTunes operate in the music and entertainment distribution industry.

First, let's examine the FYE conventional retail model. The latest movies and albums line the walls and shelves of the store. Even some hard-to-find re-mastered collections are stocked. A consumer can walk in, browse the selection, and purchase. In this model, the CD and DVD manufacturers produce what they *anticipate* consumers will

78

want to buy. The inventory is pushed to the local retail store. FYE carries the inventory until purchased by the consumer. Yet, at any point in time, FYE is full of products for which the entity has purchased in hopes of reselling for a profit. The risk in owning this unsold inventory is that no agreement exists between the current owner of the inventory (FYE) and the consumer regarding the purchase of the goods. Therefore, the producer is producing material in anticipation of customer demand, not in reaction to it. Due to the time it takes to advertise, produce, package, and ship the CDs and DVDs, retailers are left with little choice but to incur the risk associated with the inventory. We know intuitively that the inventory risk and associated carrying costs of the inventory are reflected in the sales price of the merchandise. This retail process, while pragmatic, lacks elegance due to the enormous amount of waste the producer incurred in order to bring selection and convenience to the consumer.

Consider the process elegance of iTunes. Browsing online from any location in the world makes "shopping" very convenient. Once the music or movie is selected and paid for, it can be downloaded directly. From the consumer's perspective, iTunes provides entertainment on-demand, offering its products whenever, wherever they are wanted. The concept of inventory takes on a new meaning in the iTunes model. There are not thousands of CDs lining walls and shelves, only terabytes of storage space housing the original music files.

Note the significant difference between these two models. In traditional retail, inventory is pushed to the consumer via the physical distribution channels. In the online experience, the product is pulled at will by the consumer. The iTunes model provides benefit to both the consumer and the producer as it minimizes most of the TIM WOOD waste. These pull systems allow the consumer to choose directly from a portfolio of offerings, satisfying the consumer's need for selection and convenience. The producer also benefits because the delivery processes closely match the consumer pull, substantially mitigating the risk of over-production and inventory.

It is not always possible to have a pure on-demand delivery system. Technology costs may be prohibitive or the value of the product or service may be in the customization it offers. Regardless, the principle of matching the tempos of consumer demand and the producer's process provides mutual benefit. Precisely triggered and timed processes reduce the consumer's wait time and the producer's inventory, increasing the overall value of the exchange for both parties.

Chapter 9: Get Rhythm, Part 2 – Synchronicity

"Dance with the one that brung ya."

The second aspect of rhythm is synchronicity, or the extent to which the moving parts of the process operate simultaneously. My family and I attended two very different musical events in the past year. The first was a concert featuring our daughter's favorite band. This event gave me the opportunity to experience what it was like to be amid twenty-three thousand screaming girls (and their mothers). While not the Beatles, the talented group provided great and memorable entertainment. Their fans appreciated the band's up-tempo and synchronous musical style.

I contrast this with the local elementary school band – a group of children just learning to play their instruments. Under the direction of the bandleader, the tempo of the group remained somewhat constant. Each individual child carefully concentrated on every note with unmatched intensity to the best of their ability. However, as a group, the band lacked synchronicity. Some played a little too fast, some played a little too slow, but on average, the tempo was what one might expect for the selection being played. The asynchronous nature of the children's band made it nearly unbearable to listen to, much less enjoy. This analogy holds true within a process. While the tempo or cycle time of the process may on average match customer demand, each step in the process must also be timed accordingly to ensure a balanced process.

Both tempo and synchronicity work together to produce process elegance. The correct process tempo matches the producer's processes to the consumer's demand thereby minimizing waste. Synchronicity eliminates waste within the producer's processes. Asynchronous processes are plagued by a series of starts and stops along the process continuum.

Imagine a process has three tasks in which Task 1 requires fifteen minutes to complete, Task 2 requires ten minutes to complete, and Task 3 requires five minutes.

Additionally, Tasks 2 and 3 cannot begin until the previous tasks have been completed. The process can be represented in this manner.

Figure 9.1 A Three-Step, Asynchronous Process

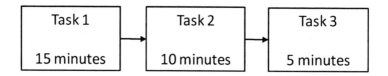

This very simple process can be described in three ways. First, the total process time is thirty minutes — the amount of time it takes to complete all the tasks in the process. Secondly, the maximum cycle time is fifteen minutes. (Task 1 is the task requiring the most time to complete.) This maximum cycle time sets the *tempo* of the process. The process can move no faster than the slowest step in the process. Thirdly, this particular process is also asynchronous, meaning each of the tasks within the process require significantly different times to complete, causing an unbalanced workload.

Suppose this process map represented how we invoice our clients. We would build up a backlog or "inventory" of unpaid work in the form of unprocessed invoices; Task 1 takes significantly longer to complete than do Tasks 2 and 3. This inventory of incomplete invoices represents lack of payment for work our business has already performed, employees we have already paid, with material we have already purchased.

To improve this process, we first need to synchronize or balance the process, distributing the work content in Tasks 1, 2, and 3 more evenly until all three tasks or sets of tasks require ten minutes to complete. Our process now could be represented as shown below.

Figure 9.2 A Three-Step, Synchronous Process

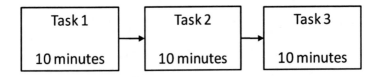

The process now exhibits a steady internal rhythm (synchronicity). It runs on a thirty-minute cycle, producing a completed work unit every ten minutes. If we are generating invoices, we can say that it takes thirty minutes to complete one invoice. We can also say that our process will complete one invoice every ten minutes with three invoices in process at any point in time.

Let's assume that billable work is being completed every eight minutes. A problem arises in that we can only process an invoice every ten minutes. Our goal must now be to reduce the ten-minute cycle time to eight minutes to match the demand for an invoice. To reduce this process time, we need to examine each of the individual tasks, looking for TIM WOOD waste-reduction opportunities. In order to sync output with demand, we must eliminate two minutes worth of waste in each of the three process steps.

In seeking to encourage a rhythm and minimize waste, it is worthwhile to ensure and maintain process balance. Balance in the process requires each of the tasks be equivalent in both time and effort to complete. In our invoice example, we achieved time balance by re-shifting work from one task to another. Consideration should also be given to the amount of effort or difficulty of each of the tasks. Even though the time component of each task is equivalent, we did not consider the complexity or skill level required to complete each task. What would happen if Task 2 were significantly more complicated than Task 1 and Task 3? The worker responsible for Task 2 would need a significantly higher skill level than the two other workers. When this type of imbalance occurs, cross-training workers becomes very difficult, if not impossible. Therefore, it is beneficial to the producer to distribute the tasks evenly according to both the time and complexity, enabling more flexibility in work assignments.

Process rhythm can bring awareness to potential process flaws. Asynchronous processes, or those unable to

THE ELEGANT PROCESS

maintain a rhythm over an extended period, tend to be obvious places to look for improvement opportunities. I was asked to evaluate a manufacturing process for ways to boost output without spending significant capital or redesigning the process entirely. The company was experiencing a period of high customer demand, selling every part it could make. They could not afford to stop production to make big changes to the process. I needed to find ways to improve output in order to satisfy the increase in demand. The assembly line was complex, highly automated with robots, conveyors, and high-tech lasers.

My first undertaking was to walk around the maze of machines with a stopwatch, carefully taking measurements of time-based process metrics. I was watching one conveyor, but a nearby machine captured my attention by its almost musical rhythm. "Kah-chunk, shhhh; kah-chunk, shhhh; kah-chunk, shhhh; kah-chunk, shhhh." The rhythm was so precise and the tempo so measured you could almost dance to it, if you were so inclined.

I watched for a minute or so, and then the machine stopped suddenly but discretely. Three seconds later, it started up again without human intervention. Now I was curious. I watched the machine for another minute. "Kah-chunk, shhhh; kah-chunk, shhhh," and again, another three-second pause. I became more intrigued. The spontaneous starts and stops

86

continued to occur every minute or so. I asked the operator why this machine stops and starts suddenly every minute. He said to me, "Yeah, it does that sometimes. Not sure why. It's no big deal. It's only for a couple of seconds." I kept my eye on this machine for the next couple of hours. It continued the start-and-stop pattern throughout the rest of the day. Researching historical records of the machine, I found that this particular machine lost its rhythm (i.e., started and stopped) almost religiously once a minute, every hour of every day. A root-cause investigation showed that the pause was caused by a flaw in the machine logic forcing it to pause under certain conditions.

I considered three very important facts. One, this machine was the slowest in a long line of machines and set the pace for the entire process. The pause in this machine caused a slowdown throughout the entire assembly line. Secondly, a three-second pause every sixty seconds is a 5% loss. The company was producing 5% fewer parts solely because of this three-second pause. Finally, the line worker did not even realize the impact of the pause. Every minute of every day, 5% of the company's revenue evaporated into thin air, and no one seemed to notice or recognize its significance. As it turned out, the fix for this pause was not as simple as flipping a switch or turning a screw. But with a little engineering work, the pause was eliminated without a huge investment or extended line shut down.

This story illustrates the powerful concept of process rhythm. The process was not overtly broken; it functioned well enough at 95%. *Yet still, the process was **waiting** on itself for three non-value-adding seconds!* This opportunity was screaming out to anyone who would listen, "Fix me! I can't keep my rhythm. Please help!" Everyone around knew about the pause but failed to acknowledge it as *waste*. Failure to recognize this as a problem resulted in a 5% reduction in sales revenue. This three-second pause compounded into an annual waste of over three million dollars. Once the pause was removed and the process rhythm restored, the company immediately began to reap the reward.

Rhythm is an indispensible concept of process development and analysis. Just as the sound of a beating human heart is an indicator of overall health, so too is the rhythm of a process. Synchronicity and tempo, both aspects of process rhythm, indicate the internal and external "health" of the process. Careful attention and analysis of these parameters provide a wealth of information on the process. When process rhythms are not carefully monitored, the process can very quickly become a random scatter of its individual tasks. Flowing, elegant processes are built to key upon specific triggers to ensure each task within the process remains in lock step with all other tasks.

A NASCAR pit crew is a great example of the value of process rhythm. During a race, racecars make routine pit stops for refueling and tire changes. When a racecar arrives in its designated pit area (the process trigger), the seven-man pit crew jumps into action. The jack man raises the left side of the car while two tire changers remove the lug nuts. New tires are handed to the tire changers by two tire carriers. Once removed, the tires are wheeled away by the tire carriers and two more new tires are brought back to the racecar. Once the left-side tires are replaced, this sequence is repeated on the right side of the car. While all this is going on, two other crewmembers are filling the racecar with gasoline and making minor adjustments to the vehicle. The entire pit stop lasts just thirteen seconds! This elegant process flows with precision. The thirteen-second pit stop is the result of rhythm — each crewmember performing his job in the prescribed amount of time. The successful pit stop requires both tempo and synchronicity to accomplish the ultimate goal of getting the racecar back on the racetrack as quickly as possible.

Business processes can operate the same way. Each member of the process team must have a defined job within the overall process. This job must be done in an exact and timely manner to ensure an optimal result. Confusion and

THE ELEGANT PROCESS

miscommunication waste time and resources, jeopardizing the goal of bringing value to the consumer. Does your team have a pit-crew mentality? Utilize the principle of process rhythm to ensure your team is as efficient and effective as it can be.

Chapter 10: Go with Flow

---

*"The quality of the imagination is to flow
and not to freeze."*

−*Ralph Waldo Emerson*

Subway, the sandwich shop, offers an interesting take on process flow. I have observed a few variations of the same model at different Subways, depending primarily on the number of associates behind the counter. But basically, the process is the same no matter which Subway I have been in. The first Subway worker in the line asks the customer what type of sandwich they would like, specifically bread, meat, and cheese. The "sandwich artist" assembles the first three ingredients and then passes the sandwich down the counter to the vegetable section where the more healthy toppings are added. The sandwich is now ready for the final touches like mayo, mustard, oil and vinegar, salt and pepper. Finally, the sandwich is wrapped up and handed to the customer. What makes this process so elegant is that the object of value (the sandwich) keeps moving throughout the process. The process begins when the customer order triggers the assembly process and it does not stop until the sandwich is in the customer's hand.

A different and less desirable strategy is used in cafeterias across the country. A limited selection of sandwiches (usually, hamburgers, chicken, and fish) are prepared in the back and sent down a metal slide and heated by four heat lamps. The customer can choose from this limited selection. If the front worker notices an empty slot where the chicken sandwiches are supposed to go, she yells to the back, "Need some chicken!" Several minutes later, half a dozen chicken sandwiches come barreling down the slide, providing an inventory of chicken sandwiches. The Subway and cafeteria models present two very different process flow methodologies.

The Subway model is described as a *continuous flow* process, meaning the sandwiches move one at a time and continuously through the value-adding process steps. Once the sandwiches receive the meat and cheese, they are immediately transferred to the vegetable section of the assembly process, then to the finish line. In the traditional cafeteria model, sandwiches are *batched* and sit in inventory until they are selected by the customer. The continuous flow process model offers several advantages over the batch process.

Continuous flow processes tend to have lower process times — the time between when the process is started and when the benefit is delivered to the consumer. The process flows to the customer sooner rather than later. Earlier, we defined value as the customer's perception of benefit relative to the customer's investment of time and money. If we can then get the same benefit to the consumer quicker, the value to the consumer is increased. In the case of the Subway sandwich, from the time the bread is pulled from the oven until the time the sandwich is handed to the consumer is about ninety seconds. Thus, the consumer buys a sandwich that is approximately ninety seconds old.

In the cafeteria model, when a fresh batch of sandwiches is put out under the heat lamp, the "age" of the sandwich depends on the size of the batch compared to the rate of consumer demand for the particular type of sandwich. Imagine while one sandwich is under the heat warmer, the cook decides to deliver a batch of five more sandwiches for a

THE ELEGANT PROCESS

total of six sandwiches in the queue. As customers arrive, they select a sandwich at a rate of one sandwich every two minutes. The customer who picks up sandwich number six gets the sandwich that is twelve minutes old. Utilizing continuous flow allows the benefit to move through the process to the consumer in a more expeditious manner compared to the traditional "batch and sell" delivery model. Figure 10.1 illustrates the time and waste difference between these two delivery models.

Figure 10.1 Batch Versus Continuous Flow Process

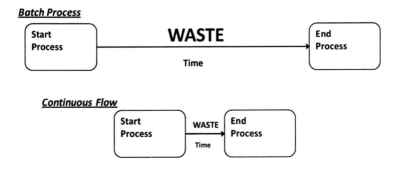

The producer also has reduced risk with continuous flow. For example, the cafeteria sandwich model contains inventory risk — risk of the sandwiches getting cold or stale, risk of the sandwiches not selling, risk of not having exactly what the consumer wants (hold the pickles, please!). We identified inventory as a type of waste in Chapter 5. Because the full cost of the work unit is contained within a completed sandwich sitting under the heat lamp, the producer's labor and material costs are sitting there motionless. This is akin to having money sitting in a savings account, drawing no interest. Idle inventory does not create value.

Inventory presents another problem. If consumers decide they no longer want chicken sandwiches, but decide they want cheeseburgers, the existing chicken sandwiches will become obsolete and must be replaced by cheeseburgers. Compare the cafeteria batch process to the Subway model. By having all the ingredients separated into smaller individual bins and by building the sandwich on demand, the Subway owner's risk is limited to the consumer's preference on the individual ingredients. If consumers opt for turkey and have no interest in ham, the Subway owner's risk is limited to the small amount of ham inventory on the serving line. The other ingredients are still good for use in all other types of sandwiches. By utilizing continuous flow, the Subway model is able to offer a wide variety of sandwich types with lower incremental risk than what would be incurred if the cafeteria chose to expand its selection of sandwich types.

In designing a new process or rebuilding old ones, thought should always be given to continuous flow principles. Ideally, continuous flow offers the quicker and lower-risk alternatives to batch process design. Though continuous process flow offers several advantages, it may not always be practical or feasible to design fully continuous processes; for example, work may require batching based on the specialty of labor required to complete the various tasks.

If we were to build a house using continuous flow principles, we would hire a small group of workers who could build the house from the foundation up. Every couple of hours, raw materials would be delivered to the job site where the same set of workers would work all day, every day on the house. Once the foundation was laid, the workers would move to framing and roofing. Then, the same workers could start the exterior before moving on to the plumbing and electrical work, sheet rock, insulation, trim, painting, carpet, and so on. This model becomes somewhat impractical based on the transportation costs required to bring in materials continuously and the expense associated with hiring and maintaining a highly skilled jack-of-all-trades workforce. It would be extremely difficult to hire a workforce that is truly efficient and has expertise in all areas of home construction. Thus, a compromise between batching and continuous flow must be reached by dividing work according to specialty and delivering the required materials just in time to minimize the risk of loss or damage. We expect the workforce to be competent within its specialty to perform all varieties of tasks within that specialty. It would be grossly inefficient to have one painting crew dedicated to painting walls, another to painting doors and windows, and a third to staining and sealing woodwork.

Despite this tradeoff, the principle of continuous flow still holds true. As handoffs between crews can be reduced and more work can be done by a fewer number of people, continuous flow improves throughout the building process. Even with some batching, efficiency gains can be made by utilizing a more broadly skilled and flexible workforce, reducing the number of specialties required to complete the job. If, for example, we had an exterior crew responsible for the foundation, frame, roof, brickwork, windows, and doors and we had an interior crew responsible for plumbing, electric, insulation, sheetrock, and painting, we could simplify the ordering, delivery, payroll, and supervisory processes. Simplifying these functions reduce overhead costs and the number of exchanges between work crews. It may not always be possible to take such a quantum leap, but the consideration of such strategies and the analysis of waste-reduction opportunities inevitably lead to improvement opportunities.

In my experience, the principle of continuous flow is the most often ignored, misunderstood, and heavily debated of all the principles set forth in this book. The natural tendency is to batch work under the assumption that batching allows workers to focus on a particular task rather than on a series of tasks. And by focusing workers' efforts on an individual task, efficiency is gained by the worker continuously repeating the same task. This is the view of some.

I would offer a different view. By segmenting work and batching tasks, workers become bored, easily distracted, and lose sight of the importance of their work. In addition, segmenting work in this manner requires additional transportation of work among workers and creates *inventory* or batches of work between each worker. Most business tasks are not so specialized or intricate that one well-trained worker cannot competently complete a series of varied tasks. Moving toward a continuous flow process actually reduces effort while keeping the workforce mentally engaged in delivering value to the consumer.

Consider a scenario that could easily occur within a physician's practice. Three physicians work in the same office. The majority of the revenue comes from insurance payments, which require a three-step process for applying for this reimbursement. The service must be documented and patient information verified. The documented service must be converted to a charge code. The charge code must be submitted to the insurance company for reimbursement.

GO WITH FLOW

In this office, Doctors Smith, Jones, and Brown keep a full schedule seeing patients. The office staff, Mary, Pam, and James, are responsible for ensuring claims are submitted on behalf of the patients. At the end of every day, the doctors give Mary all the patient documentation from the day's work. The next morning, Mary begins to verify that all necessary documentation is present and verifies the patient information is correct. At the end of the day, after Mary completes the paperwork, she passes the stack to Pam. The next day, Pam reviews the documentation and converts the services provided by the physician into codes as required by the insurance company. On the following day, Pam passes the stack of papers to James who enters the data into the computer and tracks receipt of the payments. Figure 10.2 illustrates this four-day process.

Figure 10.2 Four-Day Batch Process

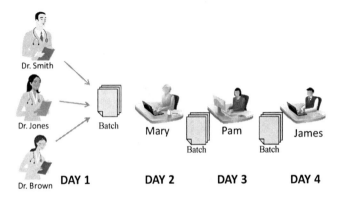

99

This is a typical example of batching. The batch size is a day's worth of work and each worker does the same thing every day. Batching work presents several risks to the practice. Any complication or disruption in the first task causes the entire process to slow or halt. The process also necessitates a four-day waiting period while the documents make their way through the process. If the office operates twenty days per month, four days of waiting represents 25% of the practice's revenue (four-day process/twenty total days) sitting in queue, waiting to be submitted to the insurance company. In essence, 25% of the practice's revenue is sitting on the staff's desks at all times.

An alternative model to this process would be to designate Mary, Pam, and James to a specific physician. In this process, Mary, Pam, and James would each be responsible for the complete billing cycle for their respective doctor. This strategy requires Mary, Pam, and James to cross-train, ensuring each could competently perform all payment processing tasks. Upon receipt of the documents from the doctor, Mary, Pam, and James would process each patient's paperwork entirely before proceeding to the next patient's record. Furthermore, if each physician forwarded the documentation immediately following each patient visit, then Mary, Pam, and James' workflows would be in complete rhythm with the physicians' rendering of services. This continuous flow process is illustrated in Figure 10.3.

Figure 10.3 One-Day Continuous Flow Process

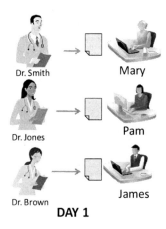

If the physicians are consistent in delivering the documentation to the payment processors, the time delay between the physician's service and the submission would be reduced to one hour or less. Instead of 25% of the entire practice's revenue sitting in an inventory of paperwork, only about 2% of the revenue would be in process at any given point in time (one hour delivery times three doctors divided by 160 hours per month = 1.9%).

Again, the continuous flow model is an ideal process scenario. In most cases, it is highly advantageous to implement such a strategy. Oftentimes, continuous flow is

THE ELEGANT PROCESS

not utilized under the assumption that it is too difficult or complicated, or that it provides no real advantage. Not implementing continuous flow based on the assumption that workers cannot be cross-trained or tasks are not synchronous is somewhat of an excuse to maintain the status quo. The benefit of the continuous flow method is in the constant transformation of the work-in-process asset into cash. The sooner this transformation into cash takes place, the lower the risk to the producer.

Continuous flow processes also allow the producer to start and stop the process based on consumer demand triggers. The ability to quickly ramp up and ramp down the process reduces labor cost, excess inventory, and the potential for defects. Effective gains made by utilizing continuous flow are typically more difficult to implement than establishing a process rhythm; however, the two are linked. The ability of the process to start and stop in step with demand, combined with the ability to convert work-in-process quickly into cash leaves the producer with a highly efficient and lower-cost process.

Chapter 11: Error-proof the Process

"Anyone who has never made a mistake
has never tried anything new."

–Albert Einstein

Once the basic framework of the process is in place, certain precautions must be taken in order to error-proof the process. I had an office located on the second floor of our corporate training and conference center. The lower level of this facility was used to host events and had several amenities, which included an industrial coffee-maker. Under normal circumstances, one of the conference center staff members would arrive early to make the coffee.

103

THE ELEGANT PROCESS

Brewing coffee in an industrial coffeemaker is similar to making coffee at home. But unlike household coffeemakers, this industrial coffeemaker supplies its own water as it is plumbed directly into the water line. To make coffee using the industrial coffeemaker, simply position the filter, add coffee grounds, and press the start button. It was simple enough if the instructions were followed.

There was an ongoing problem, however. If a meeting started before the conference center staff arrived, a meeting attendee would likely try to help out and attempt to make the coffee. On top of this particular model of industrial coffeemaker was a service access panel secured by a thumbscrew. More often than not, the unsuspecting meeting attendee would mistake the thumbscrew for a knob and open the access panel. Despite the warning sign and the posted directions, the well-intentioned attendee would make the mistake of pouring a pot of fresh water into the top of the coffeemaker, similar to what one would do at home, not realizing the coffeemaker did not require an external water source. Once the start button was pressed, the coffeemaker would supply its own water, thus overfilling itself and spilling water onto the surrounding counter and floors. If left long enough to reach its brewing cycle, the coffeemaker would also overfill the coffee pot, covering the surrounding surfaces with coffee. This mistake was repeated over and over again

104

despite the numerous signs and warnings about not pouring water into the coffeemaker.

One day, one of my colleagues suggested we make a laminated sign and tape it directly to the access panel. I suggested, as evidenced by the number of placards already in place, that an additional sign was unlikely to be an effective error-proofing technique. From an error-proofing standpoint, signage is only effective if it is read, understood, and followed. The root cause of the problem was the confusion generated by the thumbscrew looking like a knob.

We are conditioned to believe that knobs are made to be turned or pulled in some way and their mere presence suggests action is required. The presence of the "knob" was counterintuitive to the desired process. The correct process required no action while the "knob" suggested otherwise. The solution was not an additional sign; it was to replace the knob-like thumbscrew with a fastener type not having an intuitive call for action. For fifteen cents we were able to purchase a stainless steel button head screw. The knob-like thumbscrew was replaced by the lower-profile and less prominent button head screw. This solution still allowed the maintenance staff to access, clean, or repair the coffeemaker as required, without giving a knob-like appearance to the casual observer. Since that simple change, we never had to clean up overflow water or coffee again.

Figure 11.1 Example of a Thumbscrew and a Button Head Screw

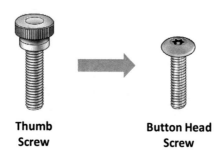

Thumb Screw   Button Head Screw

Error-proofing requires that each task within the process be carefully critiqued and evaluated on the likelihood of the task being performed correctly. Based on that evaluation, if an unacceptable likelihood for errors exists, countermeasures should be built into the process to prevent the mistake from occurring.

You may have heard the term *idiot-proofing* used to describe the concept of *error-proofing*. It should be pointed out that the two are not the same. The term *idiot-proofing*, no doubt, arose to describe an attempt to prevent the unintended consequences of poor decision-making by the uninformed. However, *error-proofing* is a proactive attempt to prevent the process from allowing otherwise likely mistakes.

Typically, errors occur when competent workers make reasonable mistakes, because of the lack of process controls in place, as was the case with the coffeemaker. On the other end of the spectrum are those who lack the skill set to perform the basic process functions and defy all logic in performing their work. This is a personnel issue and should not be confused with a process issue. I am convinced, however, of the ability of a competent workforce to perform the tasks of an elegantly designed process without ongoing errors.

Two parameters should be considered when deciding what level of error-proofing is required for a specific task within the process, which are (1) *the probability of a failure occurring* and (2) *the severity of the consequences if it does.* Probability is an estimate based on prospective analysis or empirical data of the likelihood the task will not be performed correctly. Many factors can go into estimating probability, which include complexity of the task, skill level of the workers, number of decision points, and level of automation. ***Chapter 7: Shrink the Process*** addresses this topic indirectly. It is wise to compress the process as much as possible before attempting to error-proof the process. By shrinking the process first, the number of countermeasures required to ensure robustness is kept low. Error-proofing is not typically a cost-neutral proposition; thus, applying the principles from Chapter 7 reduces both the probability of failure and the cost of error-proofing.

For most process designs, probability of failure can be applied using a simple approach. On a relative scale of one to five, determine how difficult or complicated each of the tasks

THE ELEGANT PROCESS

is. The most difficult task or process step within the process can be assigned a value of five. By assigning a task a complexity level of five, we are assuming a high probability of this task being performed incorrectly. Based on five being the most problematic, we can rank the probability level of the remaining tasks, with the easiest, simplest task being assigned a value of one. Never assign a zero to a task (you will see why in a few minutes).

One suggestion is to assign these probability values as a team of three to six people. This ensures cross-functional representation and a variety of opinions. What is easy or simple to one may not be to another. Having a range of opinions, skill levels, and experience is helpful in providing an insightful evaluation of the process.

Take, for example, the process of estimating the cost of installing a new outdoor deck. The process involves gaining customer agreement on the work, estimating the size and cost of the proposed deck, and delivering a written estimate to the customer. For each one of the steps in the process, I have assigned a relative level of difficulty in completing each task *correctly*. For risk analysis purposes, we can assume all the process steps are independent of each other. (In Step 5, where costs are calculated, we will assume the risk is in the calculation, not in whether the inputs used

108

ERROR-PROOF THE PROCESS

are correct.) In tabular form, our process risk analysis starts to take shape as Figure 11.2.

Figure 11.2 Risk Assessment Table – Assignment of Difficulty

Task / process step	Difficulty of Task (Probability)	Severity of a Failure (Severity)	Cumulative Risk
1. Gain owner agreement on design, size, and shape of deck	4		
2. Estimate size and square footage of structure	3		
3. Determine amount and cost of supplies required	4		
4. Determine number of labor hours required	5		
5. Calculate total cost, including profit	2		
6. Provide written, firm estimate to consumer	1		

The next step is to determine how critical the process step is to the output of the process. The output of this process is a written estimate that exactly represents the cost and profit expected from building the deck. In the context of this estimating process, the worst outcome would be to lose money on the job. Therefore, those process steps that represent the opportunity to lose money on the project are given a severity of five. The second-worst outcome would be the consumer deciding not to proceed with the job. Losing the

109

THE ELEGANT PROCESS

job entirely is not desirable, but it is not as severe as getting the job but losing money on it. So for this possible outcome, we could assign a severity of four. Finally, for those process failures potentially leading to an inconvenience or requiring a minor recovery effort, I have assigned a severity level of three. Adding these values to the matrix, we are left with estimates for both probability and severity as shown in Figure 11.3.

Figure 11.3 Risk Assessment Table – Assignment of Severity

Task / process step	Difficulty of Task (Probability)	Severity of a Failure (Severity)	Cumulative Risk
1. Gain owner agreement on design, size, and shape of deck	4	4	
2. Estimate size and square footage of structure	3	3	
3. Determine amount and cost of supplies required	4	3	
4. Determine number of labor hours required	5	5	
5. Calculate total cost, including profit	2	5	
6. Provide written, firm estimate to consumer	1	5	

In order to gain a clearer picture of the total cumulative risk in each process, we multiply the values assigned to probability and severity to produce the cumulative risk of the process step. The highest numbers indicate high-risk process steps. The cumulative risk number provides a ranking mechanism on which to base error-proofing decisions. Error-proofing consideration should be given first to the highest risk items, followed by analysis in descending order of the remaining items. The following completed table (shown as Figure 11.4) outlines the risks and sets forth a prioritization for reducing risk through error-proofing.

Figure 11.4 Risk Assessment Table – Cumulative Risk Calculation

Task / process step	Difficulty of Task (Probability)	Severity of a Failure (Severity)	Cumulative Risk
1. Gain owner agreement on design, size, and shape of deck	4	4	16
2. Estimate size and square footage of structure	3	3	9
3. Determine amount and cost of supplies required	4	3	12
4. Determine number of labor hours required	5	5	25
5. Calculate total cost, including profit	2	5	10
6. Provide written, firm estimate to consumer	1	5	5

We have determined our highest risk process step is estimating the labor required to build the deck. Labor cost estimation is the most unknown variable and presents the

111

greatest opportunity to produce a bad result (defect) in the form of a less than actual cost estimate. Based on this analysis, the priority will be to develop process controls to minimize the risk of underestimating labor costs.

In reality, this entire estimating process does not have the luxury of time. An estimate must be given to the customer quickly, preferably on the spot. The value in creating the estimate is lost if it requires spending hours or days ensuring a precise labor estimate. The process must include a method to quickly calculate an accurate labor estimate as well as a safeguarding mechanism that ensures an expeditious turn-around time.

One workable solution is to have predefined labor standards or formulas based on the most reliable metric or process derivative available. Square footage and number of supports may be easily projected from Steps 1 and 2. A straightforward formula can be derived to quickly estimate how much labor is required to complete the job based on the number of square feet and flooring supports that are needed to build the deck. This is only possible if sufficient and reliable data exists on past deck installations. If it does, this method becomes a reliable error-proofing mechanism for this type of process. If necessary baseline information does not currently exist, the builder must put a plan in place quickly to track and measure labor cost as a function of square footage and number of supports on all future projects. This data can be used to develop the future estimation formula.

The most appropriate error-proofing strategy is wholly dependent on the nature of the process. Methods can vary based on the potential risk contained in the process and are often subject to cost and time constraints. Error-proofing is not generally free of charge and requires some level of time investment. Also be cognizant that excessive error-proofing can inadvertently increase process time and complexity, counteracting its original intent. Judicious application of error-proofing to those high-risk sub-processes is most important.

Simpler error-proofing strategies have less of a chance to break down, deteriorate, or fail and thus can serve more reliably than complicated strategies. More sophisticated techniques should only be used when absolutely necessary and where a simple solution cannot be found.

Governance is also an important error-proofing consideration. The term *governance* refers to the level of difficulty required to short-circuit a process control. A governed process is one in which it is very difficult to bypass the error-proofing. If the error-proofing strategy is easy and advantageous for the workforce to navigate around, it becomes ineffective due to the lack of governance. I am not proposing a police state in the office, complete with

THE ELEGANT PROCESS

uniformed hall monitors and quality inspectors. Rather, I am pointing out that the most effective error-proofing techniques are self-governed, *meaning the process cannot advance unless the preceding steps are done correctly.* Self-governed processes are designed as fail-safe mechanisms, shutting down the process rather than allowing it to proceed incorrectly.

The fundamental question regarding error-proofing and governance of a process is this: "Is it easier for the worker to do his or her work correctly or incorrectly?" If the answer is "incorrectly," the process has not yet been fully developed and remains inadequately error-proofed. Work on the process design must continue until the process becomes decidedly accommodating to those performing the tasks. If those doing the work are not completely convinced and satisfied with the process design, there will always be a tendency to shortcut the processes, leaving the desired outcomes in jeopardy. These shortcuts inevitably lead to one or more of the seven wastes.

Poorly designed processes tend to fail frequently for which the workforce is usually and undeservedly blamed. Continued process failures are an obvious indication of over-complexity and an out-of-control process. These failures cost time, money, and customer loyalty and are often the difference between businesses thriving or barely surviving.

114

Chapter 12: Technology and the Visual Workplace

"Technology allows us to make the same mistakes, only faster!"

– Len Calabrese

Technology is often and mistakenly looked upon as a substitute for process design. Applying slick technology to a poorly designed process will not miraculously create a new and elegant process. As my friend, colleague, and retired Eastman Kodak executive Len Calabrese puts it, *"Technology allows us to make the same mistakes, only faster!"* Golfers are notoriously famous for

115

THE ELEGANT PROCESS

proving this point. A couple of years ago, I took up the game of golf. My dad gave me a set of golf clubs that were several years old. For weeks, I went to the driving range and whacked, hacked, and dug trenches, trying to hit the ball with these clubs. I made the [false] assumption that these old clubs lacked the technology required to (a) hit the ball, and (b) hit it straight. Ignoring the obvious, I acquired the latest and greatest golf clubs. I proudly carried my new bag of clubs out to the driving range and began to swing away, only to be out-driven by the eight-year-old girl next to me. Humiliated, I signed up for **private** lessons. Within a month, I could hit the ball solidly and occasionally even hit it straight. I learned a very valuable lesson about technology versus process control, proving Len's point. My problem was not the golf clubs (technology), it was my swing (process).

Contrast my golf club experiment with the airline ticket example given in Chapter 1. The electronic method of purchasing a ticket was an enhancement to a mature and reliable process, not a quick fix to an inherently broken process. The electronic process was developed to address the very specific issues related to variations in wait time and labor costs contained within the older version. The electronic process was implemented to reduce costs by putting the flight time research and ticket purchase into the hands of the consumer. Electronic ticketing was not a response to travel

116

agents and customer service representatives being unable to process requests correctly. Technology was used to advance the process to a more desirable state, streamlining the manual aspects, while retaining the robust nature of the original manual process.

Technology does, however, play a prominent role in process design. It offers a sizable return on investment if leveraged properly. The early stages of technology integration should focus on process measurement and feedback. This use of technology, referred to as the Visual Workplace, includes the ability to effectively measure, analyze, and display key process characteristics. This should be the initial phase and foundation of technology application.

Well-known, existing technology is a facilitator of an elegant process. The advantages of such technology application became clear to me on one project in particular. The client managed a large assembly line. But because it was so large, it lacked a sense of ownership and purpose by those workers charged with running it. The multi-million dollar question was how to make a cultural shift from one large, ominous, and often intimidating process to a series of smaller, manageable sub-processes. The line is represented generically in Figure 12.1.

Figure 12.1 Representation of a Large Assembly Line

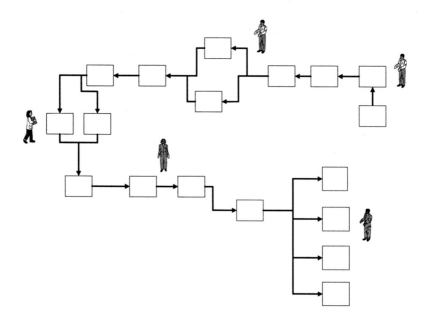

The first step was to divide this mammoth process into five zones. Each zone represented an equivalent level of complexity and effort on the part of the workers. Workers were assigned to a zone along the process continuum. The Visual Workplace concept was applied at the zone level rather than at the task level (micro-level) or the process level (macro-level). The worker in each zone, now referred to as the *owner* of the zone, was asked what information was needed from the downstream zone and what information was needed from the current zone in order to perform the work more effectively. The effort of seeking out input from the zone owners created a sense of vendor/customer relationships among the workers. Each owner became the proprietor of his or her zone, both expecting from the downstream vendor and striving to deliver to the upstream customer. This represented a significant cultural shift in the way each person viewed his or her colleague. They became more than just co-workers; they became interdependent on each other and accountable to each other. The figure below represents how the owners assumed responsibility of their respective zone.

Figure 12.2 Zoning of the Assembly Line

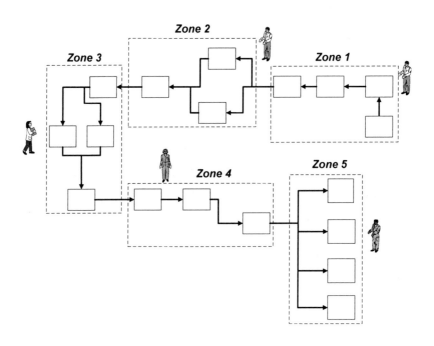

THE ELEGANT PROCESS

Technology was then used to collect the requested information unique to the preference of each zone owner. This information was electronically digested, analyzed, and displayed to the zone owner via LCD display, conveniently located as decided by the owner. As the use of this technology evolved, owners had input over all aspects of the information being transmitted to their zone. It communicated relevant information from sources both upstream and downstream, offered feedback to the owner on his or her zone by highlighting areas within the zone experiencing difficulty and needing attention.

This application of technology did not replace or redefine the actual process. It merely enhanced it by providing a measurement and feedback system within the existing context. Because information was provided back to the owner in real-time, it empowered the owner to make decisions about the zone as if it were his or her own small business, responsible for the "acquisition" and "resale" of product passing through their zone. This created new sub-processes within the overall process and simplified the human-to-machine management interface as shown in Figure 12.3.

120

Figure 12. 3 Virtual Effect "Visual Workplace" Implementation

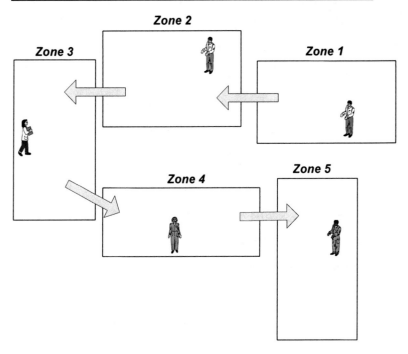

The Visual Workplace concept permeated to other aspects of the business as well. Work instructions transitioned from "how-to manuals" comprised of thousands of typewritten pages to one-page visual cues containing only the most relevant information. The one-page guides were posted discretely at the point of use as a continued resource for the owners, cutting down on the time to hunt and search for information. Interactive trouble-shooting guides also grew from this concept. Using basic web-based technology, the team developed quick-reference resource material on the details of their zone available 24/7.

The technology utilized in this project had existed for some time and was thus cost-effective, reliable, and readily accepted by the organization. The uniqueness was in the application and execution of the technology in a meaningful way. It posed little risk to the desired process outcomes as it did not redirect or unduly influence the basic process functions. Through the creative use of existing technology, what was once a large, daunting mega-process became a series of manageable work zones stepping to a common rhythm to form a more elegant process. This is an example of the preferred transition to a technology-based process. Once the Visual Workplace concept is implemented, complete with measurement and feedback functionality, the process becomes a candidate for more advanced technology elements, such as automation and systems integration.

The initial phase of technology application should be used to improve the existing process rather than as a gateway to process-defining automation. Using technology to assess rather than drive process is a safer route to take and avoids jumping headfirst into the shallow end of the technology pool.

A number of arguments can be made for delaying process-defining technology purchases until the process design is healthy. This is not to disparage the role of technology in the modern workplace, but only to put it into

TECHNOLOGY AND THE VISUAL WORKPLACE

the proper context as it relates to process design. Technology is an enabler of elegant process, not an arbiter of it. The following ideas are put forth in consideration of whether it is the right time to invest in new or emerging technology.

1. New technology can pose reliability risk. The anticipated gains of new technology integration can quickly vanish if it is unreliable, lacks support, or fails to meet expectations. Large-scale integrations can fail if either the provider or the consumer lacks a complete understanding of the product and process interface. Failure to have a workable process prior to technology implementation creates a gap between expectation and outcome, leaving the process owner empty-handed.

2. New technology is often more expensive. There is a price to having the latest and greatest technology. If a process is truly elegant and technology is being applied as an enhancement, consideration should at least be given to more mature, more reliable, and lower-cost technology.

3. New technology requires a steep learning curve. Using technology to replace a faulty

123

THE ELEGANT PROCESS

process requires an overly aggressive paradigm shift within the organization. Not only must workers learn a new software or technology application, they must also learn and embrace a new process entirely. Learning new technology and a new process can quickly frustrate the workforce. Culturally, this poses significant challenges in having to shape behavior and integrate technology at the same time with limited resources.

Technology is not necessarily an automatic solution to nagging problems. Process design through the effective use of the principles in this book is the foundation to robust outcomes. Technology is a well-suited addition to a robust process for the purpose of enhancing quality and reducing cost. But technology alone is often not the remedy for a broken process. Just remember, "Think process first, then technology."

Chapter 13: The Ideal Process

"Even if you are on the right track,
you'll get run over if you just sit there."

−Will Rogers

The achievable goal is to take these principles of process design and combine the elements into a living, breathing, and workable solution to create continual and sustainable improvement. Flow, rhythm, compression, error-proofing, and technology all work together to form the elegant process. The elegant process is unique to your value stream and requires tailoring and customizing to deliver value to the consumer while enhancing quality and reducing costs.

Producing the final elegant process requires planning and evaluation proportional to the size of the project. This can be accomplished in a relatively straightforward fashion using a concept I call the *ideal process*. The *ideal process* is the most effective, theoretically possible process that flows value to the consumer according to the principles laid forth in the preceding chapters. This ideal process delivers maximum value to the consumer including only those steps absolutely necessary to accomplish the task. The ideal process is just that — ideal. It is the theoretical best-case scenario, setting the standard for the practical and hopefully elegant process. The ideal process may not even be possible in a real-world application. However, the ideal process serves as the destination on the roadmap to achieving the elegant process.

Draw the process as it is. Typical process design or redesign involves taking a real-world problem and translating it into a map — a graphical landscape of the process as it currently exists, complete with all its imperfections, snags and failures. Discovering the problems is critical in finding and defining the process waste and gives rise to the opportunity for improvement. Knowing the state of the current process, identifying its failures, and understanding how the value flows from producer to consumer are the key elements extracted from this exercise. The value stream

126

dictates the paths we will take in our process and the choices we will make in designing the elegant process.

It is perfectly acceptable, if not advisable to draw this process map using the old-fashion method of pencil and paper. This manual approach forces an intuitive and subconscious analysis of the process while allowing a complete view not always available by drafting the process on a computer screen. Another option is to map the process out on a large surface such as a table or wall, using a Post-it note for each process step. This allows for quickly adding steps or re-sequencing steps as needed. A current process map could take on this appearance in which boxes represent tasks or sub-process and diamonds represent key decision points.

Figure 13.1 Current Process Example

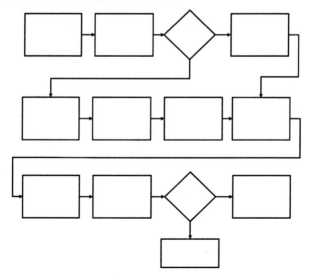

Once the process is physically drawn out, each process step must be compared against the seven TIM WOOD wastes. Each step should be color-coded into one of four categories: abnormal (rarely happens, and when it does, it's a bad thing), value-adding (consumer finds value in it), supporting (it enables the value-adding step), and avoidable (it brings no value to the process). Once this is complete, put the current process map aside and continue to the next step.

Design the ideal process. The process must deliver to the consumer the exact product or service when and where it is required. The ideal process is dictated by the consumer requirements. We must understand the time constraints and economic conditions placed on the process by the consumer and deliver the value consistent to those parameters. Envisioning the ideal process forces us to consider the most important and value delivery elements in our process design. With this in mind, I recommend sketching out the ideal process in a similar fashion as was done when drawing the current process. The ideal process should incorporate most if not all the principles described in the preceding chapters and should contain only the most necessary steps. Sketching the ideal value stream produces a gold standard with which to compare our future solution. A physical depiction of the ideal process aids in communicating to the team both the value to the consumer and the benefit to the producer of a well-

128

defined, effective, and efficient process. The goal is to develop a workable process that mirrors our ideal process to every extent possible. The ideal process map should appear to be a much simpler process with fewer steps. It should only describe the "what" and "when" of the process — which tasks are to be completed and in what order. It is not an instruction on *how* to complete the process.

Figure 13.2 Ideal Process Example

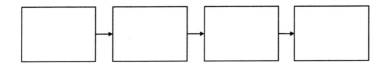

Notice the ideal process map is much more compact than the actual process map. This is why it is called *ideal*. The ideal process map defines the starting and ending points with the minimal number of process steps in between, yet still delivers the value to the consumer.

Decide what to change. By comparing the current process to the ideal process, ideas emerge on how to craft the elegant future process. Deciding how to reshape the process is the most basic and difficult undertaking. Figuring out how to simultaneously deliver the value to the consumer while minimizing or eliminating non-value-adding steps is a chore. Consider the principles of flow, rhythm, number of steps, and the proper use of technology. Combining these elements into

THE ELEGANT PROCESS

an efficient process is an important technique in building quality into the process. Quality matched with efficient flow produces a cost-effective process meeting the needs of both the consumer and producer.

I am very impressed with the efficiency gained in self-checkout lines at the grocery store. They are convenient, well thought out, and labor efficient. But like all processes, there is room for improvement. Why I analyze processes to this extent, I will never know, but I have found through experience three gaps between the actual self-checkout process and the ideal self-checkout process.

First, the self-checkout lines should not have a coin acceptor. The coin acceptors allow a certain population, notorious for insisting upon using exact change, to input as many coins, one at a time, to pay for groceries. This is not elegant. The second gap in the process is lack of automated check writing and acceptance. The local wholesale club has a system in place allowing the customer to hand over a blank check. The cashier inserts the check into the register and hands it back to the customer. The tab is paid via electronic fund transfer. This should be the case in self-checkout. It should either automate the check-writing process or not allow it. But allowing a customer to write a check, then requiring a photo ID and a manager's approval in order to accept the check is neither ideal nor elegant. Finally, in the category of

130

THE IDEAL PROCESS

non-elegant processes, while [patiently] waiting in the self-checkout line, I once observed a young mother trying to scan and bag her groceries with her one free arm while in the present act of feeding her baby with the other. The designers of the self-checkout process had not accounted for this scenario. Obviously, neither had the mother.

My analysis of the self-checkout process points to the necessity of regularly observing the actual process relative to the ideal process in order to identify improvement opportunities. Elegance is achieved though the continual evaluation and comparison of the actual to the ideal. By doing this, given the perspective of the elegant process principles, ideas should quickly come to mind on how to design a more efficient and effective process. Combining the no-waste elements of the ideal to the value delivery of the current will produce an entirely new and much simpler future process. This new and simpler process becomes the elegant process and is a hybrid of both the ideal and current process maps as illustrated in Figure 13.3.

Figure 13.3 Combining the Current and Ideal Processes to Produce the *Elegant Process*

The Current Process

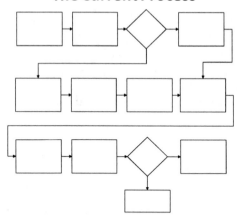

The Ideal Process

X

The Elegant Process

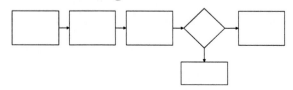

THE IDEAL PROCESS

Putting *The Elegant Process* into action

Determine to make it happen. As with all improvement activities and inspirational ideals, the question remains, "Will it stick?" Whether or not the process can be sustained depends on the usefulness of the process at all levels of the organization. If the process significantly benefits the line worker, he or she will tend to adopt and leverage it to the extent it proves beneficial. Otherwise, the improvement effort will become the "flavor of the day" and will be disregarded at the first opportunity. Similarly, management's commitment, or lack thereof, to an improved process will trickle down to all levels. To accurately project whether or not the improved process will take root within the organization, an honest evaluation of the following six considerations is encouraged:

1. *Is the new process easier than the old process?* Human nature is to find and follow the path of least resistance. Elegant processes are those processes that deliver the value with the least resistance. Ensuring the process will stick requires answering this question: "Is it easier to do it right or easier to do it wrong?" The answer to this question, in part, determines whether or not it will stick.

133

THE ELEGANT PROCESS

2. *Is the process intuitive?* This question is a complex one whose answer depends entirely on one's perspective. However, to ensure success, the process must be intuitive to the skill level of the person performing the work. What is intuitive to a highly skilled professional may not be intuitive to an entry-level worker. The purpose and flow of the elegant process must be intuitive to the skill level of the worker performing the task if it is to succeed long-term.

3. *Is the process measurable?* Outcomes that cannot be measured give no indication whether or not the process is effective. Lack of feedback on process effectiveness leaves those involved in the dark, without direction, and uncertain. However, processes designed to allow measurability and feedback to the management and workers help ensure sustainability.

4. *Is the process enforceable?* Well-designed processes are clearly documented and routinely communicated. Vague processes produce uncertainty within the workforce. Clear job responsibilities and expectations empower employees and define their professional

134

THE IDEAL PROCESS

purpose. In turn, this employee focus on that purpose ensures the long-term success of the process.

5. *Is the process appreciated?* Consider the WIIFM — "What's In It For Me?" The elegant process produces a better environment for all. I have found most hard-working people enjoy work that is productive. What drives workers crazy are the hassles stemming from broken processes. Confusion, defects, do-overs are all the result of poor process design and are highly de-motivating. Ensuring a process free of these distractions can aid in making the process stick by reinforcing an engaged workforce.

6. *Are you committed?* The most important determination you can make is this: are you committed to enhancing quality and reducing costs through the effective use of process? If so, quality becomes non-negotiable and cost-control essential. How you reinforce these beliefs will determine if the processes put in place will be sustained. Continually accepting tradeoffs between quality and cost is a formula for failure. A shrinking bottom line can tend to cause panic. The first and typical response is to wade through the business with a sickle, slashing

135

THE ELEGANT PROCESS

costs across the board. I fully recognize the necessity of doing this on rare occasions. But before getting to the "slash and burn" phase, recognize the benefit of implementing elegant processes as an insurance policy against an eroding profit margin. "Slash and burn" tends to have a negative long-term effect. If value-adding processes are cut, the consumer will suffer and become dissatisfied, resulting in lower revenue. But slashing waste and instilling the concept of process can have the same net effect without the harmful side effects.

Set your organization up for success! Build strong, effective, and efficient processes. Allow your workforce to march to the beat of a single drum. Simplify the workload of all employees by instituting robust processes across the organization. Eliminate the mistakes to improve customer satisfaction. Cost reductions come through gaining efficiency based on consumer demand. It is entirely possible by using the ideal process to develop the *elegant process*.

Chapter 14: The Way Forward

"Are you going to get any better, or is this it?"

-Manager Earl Weaver to baseball umpire.

My wife and I enjoy very few of the same television programs. She enjoys programs involving weddings, medicine, or children. I tend toward the history, engineering, or sports shows. However, there is one show we both enjoy. The show is a documentary-style series about an illness known as pathological or compulsive hoarding. The show presents stories of people who collect and store in large quantities a wide variety of items. Hoarders tend to stockpile anything

THE ELEGANT PROCESS

and everything from food or household items to clothes or animals. The condition can become so severe it often leads to bankruptcy, divorce, eviction, or child protective services stepping in. It is quite sad.

On this program, psychologists and professional organizers work with hoarders to clean, throw out trash, and organize their homes in an attempt to address and correct the behavior. If all goes well, the intervention prevents the impending consequences of the illness. What I find most interesting is that the condition produces an inability to distinguish between value and waste. Hoarders tend to assign an equally high value to every item they hoard either in recalling a memory related to the item or identifying any potential, even if obscure, use for the item. In a hoarder's mind, every item has value sufficient enough to justify keeping it forever. Businesses and organizations fall victim to the same myopia as it relates to process — an inability to distinguish between value and waste.

The challenge becomes using the principles set forth in this book as a set of lenses through which to view current processes. Lenses change our perspective, clarify our vision, and magnify our ability to see what was previously indiscernible. Upon review, instances of batching, lack of rhythm and flow, repeated mistakes, and improper use of technology can almost always be found in some form or

138

another. In many cases, we are so deeply involved in the operations that we are unable to see the process for what it is — some value, mostly waste.

I was conducting business at a local corporate office building. Walking in, I took a right, walked up two flights of stairs, and turned left to be greeted warmly by the receptionist. My colleague and I asked to see the gentleman we were to meet with. The receptionist called him and he came to get us. Following him to his office, we continued down a hallway, turned right, turned left, walked down two flights of stairs, down a hallway and to the right, finally landing in his office. The three of us joked about the maze of hallways and stairs required to get to his office. The gentleman explained to me and my colleague the history of the building. In the 1970s, the front part of the building was built to house just a few offices. As the business grew through the next thirty years, the building was modified and expanded several times, producing the inefficient floor plan we were now navigating. The building layout had unintentionally evolved over time into an overly complex design. Business processes evolve in much the same way.

Years ago, our business may have developed a hiring, invoicing, or mail-sorting process. As time crawls along, tweaks are made to the process in order to meet the immediate need. Much like the labyrinth office building,

THE ELEGANT PROCESS

these tweaks add up, creating a current process full of twists and turns. This evolution is not so much a process design effort as it is a historical record of gradual change. Because the change is so gradual and the status quo so firmly entrenched, it is often difficult to evaluate the current state of the process objectively. The tools to evaluate this *process creep* objectively and thoroughly have been laid out in the previous chapters and now form a new set of process-savvy lenses.

Process creep occurs as our customer's needs, technology, and office culture change. Our processes evolve to keep pace with the ever-changing demands on our resources. Very often, this shift does not occur in an instant, rather it can take years. The gradual shifting rarely requires a dynamic change to current processes, only minor adjustments to maintain the performance of the business. Making a convincing argument to executives about taking on a process improvement project becomes difficult. (Admittedly, they usually latch on to the cost-cutting ideas quickly!) The beauty of utilizing these process principles is their focus on two entities: waste and value. Inherently, everyone hates waste and loves value. Therefore, the concepts of waste and value are not only easily understood, but they resonate with all of us.

140

Creating a sense of urgency to deal with process issues rests in the ability to connect the dots successfully among quality and waste and cost and value. Though we understand the relationship, we may not always be able to quantify the impact of improving quality or the savings in reducing waste. Ultimately, the benefit of connecting the dots must be quantified in the universal language of dollars.

In the process examples throughout this book, I have intentionally tied process improvements to either dollars or time. Wasted time and effort is fairly easy to quantify and translate into dollars. There are three reasons why calculating this dollar value is essential in calling to action a plan for improvement. First, financial profit is the motivator in most business settings. It is either the objective or the enabler of every organization. Money measures the health and sustainability of the business, supports our lifestyle, and brings us personal security in uncertain times.

Secondly, calculating a dollar value helps prioritize resources. Suppose I were your CFO, and you asked me to choose between two projects and to provide the necessary resources for only one of them. One project proposal has quantifiable savings and impact on the organization through the reduction of process time from Point A to Point B. The second project is scoped to "unleash the human potential within our organization by leveraging our core values." It is difficult to determine which of these projects will have more of an impact on the business. With the information given in the first project, I can figure out how the success of the project will affect my bottom line. The second has a great tag line, but does not contain quantifiable measures.

In order to evaluate both projects fairly, we must determine both the cost and benefit using a common comparative. Dollars can accomplish both. Once the projects are fairly and financially evaluated, decisions can be made and resources assigned with some level of comfort.

The third reason for determining the financial impact of a project is to make a case for financial investment. Many businesses and corporations have strict guidelines on payback period, return on investment, or internal rate of return and require minimum thresholds in order to proceed with projects. Determining the financial impact in advance lends itself to anticipating or overcoming these obstacles.

I will admit that it is more difficult to assign a dollar value to improving quality. It is much easier to put a price tag on a lack of quality, as was the case in the kitchen countertops and sink example. Much more difficult is putting a dollar value to maintaining or improving existing quality. However, I do believe in estimating quality improvements in dollars for the purpose of allowing quality improvement projects to compete with cost-savings projects on an even playing field. Quality estimates are often difficult, but in most cases worth the extra effort.

By now, this book should have highlighted the ever-present need of viewing each process, each step, and each action as either adding value or creating waste. Process lenses allow us to see the business world first and foremost as a series of deliberate, measured process steps. We must practice the art and science of distinguishing between value and waste, promoting the value and eliminating the waste. As such, we are left with the constructive tension existing between the current state of the process and the ideal process. We must have the will and character to challenge what *is* in order to create what *can be*.

Creating the elegant process is much like creating a diamond; both require pressure and time to produce the valuable result. The pressure to achieve the elegant process comes in the financial reward and the personal satisfaction in delivering value to the customer in a manner that brings profit to the organization. And, of course, time — time invested in analyzing, designing, and implementing the elegant process.

The elegant process is not always free, seldom easy, but always has the same objective — to enhance quality and reduce costs.

Breinigsville, PA USA
28 December 2010
252327BV00004B/36/P